Managing in the New World of Manufacturing

How Companies Can Improve Operations to Compete Globally

GEORGE W. PLOSSL

Prentice Hall, *Englewood Cliffs, NJ 07632*

Library of Congress Cataloging-in-Publication Data

Plossl, George W., 1918–
    Managing in the new world of manufacturing : how companies can
improve operations to compete globally / George W. Plossl.
        p.   cm.
    Includes bibliographical references and index.
    ISBN 0-13-617143-5 (case)
    1. Manufactures—Management.   2. Industrial management.
3. Production management.   4. Manufactures—Technological
innovations.   5. Manufacturing processes.   I. Title.
    HD9720.5.P56   1991
    658.5—dc20   90-7906
                                                                                    CIP

Editorial production supervision and
    interior design: ELIZABETH BEST
Cover design: BRUCE KENSELAAR
Manufacturing buyer: SUSAN BRUNKE
Prepress buyer: KELLY BEHR
Page makeup: JOH LISA
Aquisitions: JOHN WILLIG

 © 1991 by Prentice-Hall, Inc.
A Simon & Schuster Company
Englewood Cliffs, New Jersey 07632

Printed in the United States of America
10 9 8 7 6 5 4 3 2 1

ISBN 0-13-617143-5

Prentice-Hall International (UK) Limited, *London*
Prentice-Hall of Australia Pty. Limited, *Sydney*
Prentice-Hall Canada Inc., *Toronto*
Prentice-Hall Hispanoamerica, S.A., *Mexico*
Prentice-Hall of India Private Limited, *New Delhi*
Prentice-Hall of Japan, Inc., *Tokyo*
Simon & Schuster Asia Pte. Ltd., *Singapore*
Editora Prentice-Hall do Brasil, Ltda., *Rio de Janeiro*

To all the professionals I have met and worked with in manufacturing operations throughout the world, which needs them more today than it ever has before.
Also to Marion, my wife, secretary, travel agent, accountant, research assistant, and chief support, without whose help none of my books would have been written.

Contents

List of Illustrations   ix

List of Principles and Strategies   x

Preface   xiii

Chapter 1   The First Law of Manufacturing Control   1

Summary, *1*
Can Manufacturing Be Controlled?, *2*
Complexity Exaggerated, *6*
The Essence of Manufacturing, *6*
Material Flow, *9*
Information Flow, *10*
Planning and Control Systems, *12*
Improving Flexibility, *13*
Theory and Practice, *15*

Chapter 2   Evolution, Facts and Fables   21

Summary, *21*
Decline of U.S. Manufacturing, *22*

Governmental Handicaps, 23
*Union Handicaps, 24   Financial Institution
Handicaps, 24   Trade Relations, 25*
Poor Management, 25
Wealth Generation and Sharing, *26*
The Evolution of Planning and Control, *28*
Inventory Fallacies and Truths, *32*
The Paradox of Inventory Control, 33
The Lead Time Syndrome, 34
The Situation Today, *36*

Chapter 3   Manufacturing as a Process   **39**

Summary, *39*
Manufacturing Is a Process, *40*
Objectives of Manufacturing, *40*
Satisfy Customers Completely, 40
Earn Adequate Profits, 42   *Use Capital
Effectively,* 42   *Generate More Wealth,* 43
Reward Participants Equitably, 43
Treat Suppliers and Customers Fairly, 43
Be a Good Citizen, 44
Differences Are Evident, *44*
Useful Classifications, *46*
Common Characteristics, *46*
Information Flow Requirements, *48*
Material Flow Requirements, *49*
Attacks on Waste, *50*

Chapter 4   Strategic Planning   **53**

Summary, *53*
The Planning Hierarchy, *54*
Strategic Planning, *57*
Useful Strategies for Design Engineering, 60
Common Marketing Strategies, 61
Strategies Applicable to Production, 61
Strategies in Finance, 62
Business Planning, *63*
Production Planning, *64*
The Production Plan and Master Production Schedule
Links, *67*
Master Production Schedules, *68*

Managements' Role in Using the Master Production
Schedules, *72*

Chapter 5 The System and Its Role   73

Summary, *73*
General Control Theory, *74*
System Objectives, *76*
Core System Elements, *77*
Subsystems, *82*
Requirements for Effective Systems, *85*

Chapter 6 Effective Execution and Control   87

Summary, *87*
Requirements for Control, *88*
    Valid Plans, 89   *Timely Feedback,* 90
    Preset Tolerances, 91   *Exception Reports,* 91
    Thorough Review, 91   *Prompt Action,* 91
Improving Internal Control, *92*
Cultural Changes Needed, *96*
    Top Management, 98   *Finance and
    Accounting,* 99   *Marketing and Sales,* 101
    Warehousing and Distribution, 102
    Design Engineering, 103   *Manufacturing
    Engineering,* 105   *Material Planning and
    Control,* 106   *Quality Control,* 108
    Production, 109   *Purchasing,* 112
    Maintenance and Plant Engineering, 113
The Changing Roles of Staff "Experts," *113*

Chapter 7 Measures of Performance   117

Summary, *117*
The Need to Challenge Tradition, *118*
    Satisfying Customers, 119   *Reducing Costs,* 120
    Reductions in Capital Requirements, 122
Decision Making with the Wrong Numbers, *122*
    Direct Labor Efficiency, 122   *Direct Material
    Costs,* 124   *Book Value of Machinery,* 125
    Return on Investment, 126
Requirements for Effective Measurement, *126*
Pysical Versus Financial Data, *128*

The Hierarchy of Performance Measurement, *129*
Financial Measures of Performance, *131*
  Inventory Turnover Rates, 131   *Return on Capital
  Employed,* 133   *Aggregate
  Production-Sales-Inventory,* 133   *Product Profit
  Margins,* 135   *Productivity,* 137
Physical measures of Performance, *138*
  Time Periods of Supply, 138   *Actual Versus
  Scheduled Output,* 138   *The Production / Delivery
  Ratio,* 139   *Number of Defects in Materials,
  Products, and Data,* 139   *Percent of Records with
  No Significant Errors,* 139   *Manufacturing Cycle
  Times,* 140   *Percent of Real Work in Cycle
  Times,* 141   *Productivity,* 142   *Number of
  Certified Suppliers,* 143   *Number of Components
  in Each Product,* 143   *Number of Bottleneck Work
  Areas,* 143   *Number of Schedules Missed,* 144
Specific Measures for Functions, *144*
Essence of Control, *146*

Chapter 8 Manufacturing in the Future   **149**

Summary, *149*
The Situation Today, *150*
Common Fallacies, *153*
  U.S. Economy Is Strong, 153
  Professional Managers Are Unprincipled, 153
  *Poor Management Is the Principle Cause of U.S.
  Decline,* 154   *U.S Productivity Still Leads
  the World,* 154   *Service Industries Will Replace
  Manufacturing,* 154   *Low-Value Dollar
  Is Needed,* 155   *Financial Games
  Are Beneficial,* 155   *Japanese Manufacturers
  Are Unbeatable,* 156
Urgent Tasks for Executives, *157*
Strategies for the Future, *159*
Hope for the Future, *165*

Bibliography   **171**

Glossary of Terms   **173**

Index   **181**

List of Illustrations

Figure No. 1–1   The Essence of Manufacturing, 7
Figure No. 1–2   Information Versus Material Speeds, 8
Figure No. 1–3   Production Cycle Management, 14

Figure No. 2–1   Evolution of Planning and Control, 28
Figure No. 2–2   How Inventory is Really Controlled, 34
Figure No. 2–3   The Lead Time Syndrome, 35

Figure No. 3–1   Manufacturing Objectives, 41
Figure No. 3–2   Complexities of Pencils, 45

Figure No. 4–1   Planning Time Relationships, 56
Figure No. 4–2   Comparison of Marketing and Production Strategies, 59
Figure No. 4–3   Typical Production Plan, 66
Figure No. 4–4   Typical Master Production Schedule, 70
Figure No. 4–5   Team or All-stars?, 71

Figure No. 5–1   Core System Elements, 78
Figure No. 5–2   Rough-cut Capacity Plan, 79
Figure No. 5–3   Typical Material Requirements Plan, 81

Figure No. 6–1   Requirements for Control, 89
Figure No. 6–2   Long Cycle Problems, 90
Figure No. 6–3   Production Cycle Time, 95

Figure No. 7–1   Customer Service Benefits, 119
Figure No. 7–2   Factory Cost Changes, 120
Figure No. 7–3   Potential Inventory Reductions, 132
Figure No. 7–4   Inventory Input/Output Report, 134
Figure No. 7–5   Product Contributions to Sales and Costs, 136
Figure No. 7–6   Manufacturing Cycle Time Elements, 141
Figure No. 7–7   Stacked Lead Times, 142

Figure No. 8–1   Profit and Loss Statement–Before, 166
Figure No. 8–2   Balance Sheet–Before, 166
Figure No. 8–3   Profit and Loss Statement–After, 167
Figure No. 8–4   Balance Sheet–After, 167

List of Principles
and Strategies

PRINCIPLES

CHAPTER 1

1. Time is the most precious resource., 10
2. The logic of manufacturing planning and control is simple and universal., 11
3. There is one system framework common to all types of manufacturing., 12
4. There is no one best way to control manufacturing., 12
5. Do not commit flexible resources to any specific item until the last possible moment., 13

CHAPTER 2

6. Well-run operations do not require complex systems., 37

CHAPTER 3

7. Manufacturing is a process involving two flows: materials and information., 47
8. No manufacturing problem is unsolvable., 49

CHAPTER 4

9. The validity of a plan increases as its horizon decreases., 72

CHAPTER 5

10. Manufacturing operations forming parts of a common process are controlled best by an integrated system., 76
11. Plans impossible to execute are the worst kind., 80, 98

CHAPTER 6

12. Replanning is the last resort; first get back on plan., 92
13. Making enough in total is a prerequisite of making the right things., 94

14. Improvements can and should be made in all functions simultaneously., 97
15. Learn to play a better game, not just keep a better score., 101
16. Know customers' real needs, not just their wants., 101
17. Sound design means much more than proper functioning., 104
18. Setting time standards is secondary to smoothing and speeding flow., 106
19. Plan only capacity requirements over long horizons; schedule specific items only in the near future., 107
20. Estimates of group totals for families of items will be more accurate than those of individual items., 107
21. Making anything too soon is a serious waste., 107
22. Input higher than output must trigger instant alerts., 108
23. Planning defines the resources needed to make what is planned; execution applies the resources available to make what customers want now., 111
24. One ace partner beats a full house of competing suppliers., 112

CHAPTER 7

25. "Data" are simply facts; "information" requires facts having useful meanings., 127
26. Ninety-five percent complete information now is far better for control than 100% later., 127
27. The best measures of performance are aggregates, not details., 128
28. Any valid control report must show both planned and actual performance data., 128
29. Physical units of measure are superior to financial., 129
30. Visual feedback is preferable to system data., 129

STRATEGIES

CHAPTER 8

1. Make education of all employees a continuous effort., 159
2. Achieve significant, continuous improvements in the performance of the business by attacking waste in all activities., 161
3. Smooth out and speed up material and information flows., 161
4. Increase the productivity of capital., 162
5. Work continuously to improve the quality of output of every business activity., 162
6. Do not commit flexible resources to any specific item until the last possible moment., 164

7. Streamline factory processes to slash inventories, material costs, and production time., 164

8. Pare management layers to force designers, engineers, production workers, and marketers to work as teams., 164

9. Harness computer technology to make small batches of customized products at low costs., 164

10. Pounce on breakthrough discoveries (like superconductivity) that will revolutionize entire businesses., 164

Preface

Some facts are obvious and widely recognized; others are obscure and visible only to a discerning eye. The decline of manufacturing in the United States illustrates both types.

The loss of many whole industries in the United States to foreign competition is obvious even to the casual observer. The dwindling global market share of others is detailed frequently in the public press.

The true causes of such losses are obscure. Many are cited. Prominent are unfair competition—restraint of trade, dumping of goods at prices below costs, and industrial espionage—low wages, government subsidies, cultural advantages, and better management. There is some truth to each of these, but a thorough analysis is not my intention in this book.

Effective action is needed soon to stop and reverse the deterioration of U.S. economic strength. Faced with such a problem, any good manager would focus on the efforts which would yield the greatest results soonest with the best chance of success. In our scenario, these are undoubtedly the actions resulting in better management of American industry.

Present executives do not necessarily have to be replaced; they need a better understanding of how manufacturing really works, what new management tools are now available and how to use them to operate in today's global competition. Like safe drivers of automobiles, they do not need volumes of highly technical information on vehicle design, maintenance, and repair. Too many of these are already in their libraries unread.

The business literature of the last decade has been markedly successful at selling books and promoting authors. It has failed abjectly, however, to stimulate improvement in the manufacturing operations on which our economic strength depends. Coining new words like megatrends and identifying the causes of excellence in a few companies (some of which soon after became not so excellent) have fallen far short of meeting the challenge. They made successes of their authors but not of their readers.

Extolling the power and glory of MRP, JIT, FMS, CIM, and many other three-letter acronyms populating the technical literature of planning and control has generated more heat than light. These have neither reached nor influenced the CEO's, presidents, managing directors, and other top-level managers who are the real culprits and, at the same time, the victims. They do not want and do not need more buzzwords, more magical mathematics, more nebulous psychological sophistication or complex concepts. They need to understand how manufacturing works and what they must do to make it work better.

In over 40 years in industry as manager, counselor, author, and lecturer working in and with many companies in every industry in all of the industrial countries in the Western world, I have seen how manufacturing can and should be run. From this experience I have attempted in this book to distill the essential nature of the manufacturing process. My purpose is to stimulate and assist executives in reversing the decline of manufacturing in the United States.

George W. Plossl

CHAPTER 1

The First Law
of Manufacturing Control

Nothing can be done or made by theory, but knowledge of theory improves the doing and making.

SUMMARY

Manufacturing is out of control in most companies. The evidence is highly visible, showing clearly managements' lack of ability to make valid plans and execute them properly. External, unavoidable factors destroy some companies, but the bulk of failures result from lack of understanding of the manufacturing process and inability to take proper actions. The machine tool industry provides some classic examples of such lack of understanding. Despite extensive loss of markets, the industry could still recover; there is little evidence that it will do so.

The complexity and uniqueness of manufacturing operations are apparent as are the amount of data needed for planning and controlling. There has been too much emphasis on techniques and buzzwords. There is a consensus that most of the myriad problems are unavoidable. This is not true.

An underlying elegance and essential simplicity exist. All manufacturing involves two flows: materials and information; both must be smoothed out and speeded up. Basic principles must be known and applied. Time is the most precious resource.

There is a universal logic underlying all manufacturing and a universal framework for planning and control systems, although there is no one best way to apply such systems. Planning, control, and execution are separate and distinct activities that need careful integration.

Flexibility is the most important characteristic of the manufacturing company with a future. Flexibility of all resources (time, money, people, materials, machines, plants, and suppliers) must be preserved until the latest possible moment.

The farther out plans extend, the less valid they will be. Shortening planning horizons by reducing cycle times requires faster and smoother flows of materials and information that result only from better balanced operations without bottlenecks.

Knowledge of theory and principles, supported by proper actions, can make significant improvements in any manufacturing company. Pessimistic prognoses of experts, based on current trends and statistical analyses, ignores this ability of people to alter the environment.

The law presented here is well tested, the principles are sound, and the techniques are uncomplicated. The prerequisites for success are known, the characteristics of successful firms are clear, and the benefits are very worthwhile. Education of executives is the most important and most difficult task.

CAN MANUFACTURING BE CONTROLLED?

Manufacturing is out of control! Shocking as it may be, this statement is true for the great bulk of companies worldwide. The word "manufacturing" as used in this book refers to businesses converting low-value materials to saleable products of higher value and includes all activities of companies engaged in this process, not just production. "Control" means the ability to make valid plans and then execute them properly. In this context it applies to relationships of a company with its suppliers and its customers as well as to its internal activities.

Major upsets, even disasters, may be caused by external happenings which are completely beyond the control of a company's management. A flood, earthquake, hurricane, fire, or explosion can wipe out a firm operating under tight and effective control. Newly discovered hazards to human health may suddenly destroy markets, as happened to Johns-Manville with asbestos. Overly zealous lawyers and weird interpretations of laws can quickly bankrupt a firm as strong as Texaco or put many companies out of business, as has happened to small airplane manufacturers. New technologies can suddenly change the nature of an industry as the resonating quartz crystal did to mechanical clocks and watches. Powerful Union Carbide was brought to its knees by sabotage coupled with failures of safety devices poorly maintained. The statement about manufacturing's being out of control does not include such happenings.

The evidence of the validity of the statement that manufacturing is out of control is all too visible. Products promised to customers, even the few best ones, are not delivered on time. Projects to introduce new products or major redesigns of current ones are not completed on time, within budgeted costs with sound designs. Major expense items are not within reasonable range of budget allowances. Quality problems are not solved. Expensive machinery is overloaded or underutilized. Materials lurch through plants instead of flowing smoothly. New customer orders or changes surprise everyone. Profit goals are missed.

Even beyond these failings, the sorry state of U.S. industry was illustrated by Robert Kuttner in a tongue-in-cheek "Economic Watch" column in the November 17, 1986 issue of *Business Week*. He used the scenario of between-innings television commercials during the baseball World Series to highlight important shortcomings. A major credit card company promoted its guarantee on items purchased using its card by showing defective tape recorders, toasters, food processors, and washing machines—common experiences for many people. This was a fine example of a service company trying to benefit from serious failures of manufacturing firms to make quality products.

A Japanese camera advertisement illustrating its innovative features was followed by an American cereal company adding another to its long list of health foods. Here was a good example of misdirected marketing efforts—hard goods getting too little and food fads getting too much attention.

Fast-food chains tout their hamburgers and toppings, now finding warm reception in the Orient. Mr. Kuttner remembered when "Americans exported industrial products while Orientals ran our fast-food restaurants." He concluded, "It almost makes you think there must be more to a successful economy than marketing genius, financial manipulation, and dizzy laissez-faire." He's so right. *There's a well-run industrial base.*

The fate of U.S. machine tool makers illustrates the results of competition when American managers who don't know how to run manufacturing come up against foreign competitors who do. In just five years during the 1980s, the latter increased share of market from 25% to over 50% and about one-third of the 500 U.S. makers went under. Tragically, that trend has continued and an industry vital to U.S. defense and wealth generation is almost lost. Pundits writing about this identify high prices and low quality as the causes; these are not the most serious ones.

I asked an executive of a client firm why they had bought two multimillion-dollar machining centers from a Japanese firm. He said that the U.S. prices were higher, but not enough to swing the sale, and that breakdowns might be higher, but repair service was nearby and responsive. The delivery time got the order for the Japanese; 9 months versus

16 months for the U.S. supplier. Much more than worker productivity accounted for this difference.

A better perspective on the competitive situation in the machine tool business was revealed in a customer's comparison of Toyoda Machine Works and Cincinnati Milacron equipment. Grading each on 44 factors on a one-to-ten scale, Toyoda got 1,425 to Milacron's 1,358 points. If this is typical, American firms still have a fighting chance—*if they accept the challenge.*

It is not yet evident that they will; one chief executive of a very prominent U.S. maker said his firm was "just hanging on." He also complained that voluntary quotas agreed to by the Japanese were too high and stated, "When you add in other imports—from countries unaffected by quotas—it doesn't leave much for U.S. producers." This is hardly aggressive "Let's go get 'em" stuff. Another major machine tool manufacturer's chief executive saw "too much machine-tool capacity in the world" and predicted a "whole series of bankruptcies around the world, including in Japan" but didn't say what his company was doing to avoid being one of them.

Anyone even remotely familiar with manufacturing is aware of the multitude of problems endemic to it. Most customers know the real truth of the statement, "The customer is always right"; they know it is true only until they have bought the products. Then it becomes evident that the products they bought

* Don't meet their real needs.
* Fail to function as claimed.
* Have a useful life shorter than desired.
* Are difficult to repair, even when parts are obtainable.
* Are sold at prices unrelated to costs.

The problems are not all on the manufacturers' side. People within manufacturing companies working directly with customers, or studying their reactions to help develop a better understanding of markets, know that customers often

* Don't know their own real needs.
* Order later than they needed to.
* Often change delivery times and quantities.
* Want more and more varieties.
* Buy lower-priced goods.
* Want only the latest models.
* When purchase contracts permit, insist on auditing all of a supplier's costs and activities.

Suppliers of goods and services to manufacturing companies have almost identical feelings about their customers.

People in manufacturing involved with procurement of materials and services know all too clearly that

* Suppliers' delivery promises are unreliable.
* Without expediting, it takes too long to get them.
* Adherence to quality standards is spotty.
* Suppliers are inflexible in reacting to changes, except for price increases.
* Other customers frequently take precedence.
* There is too little time to find better sources.

People working in production operations see evidence daily that Murphy was right—what can go wrong will, at the least opportune time. They know that

* Formal plans and budgets are unrealistic.
* New designs will be late and difficult to make.
* Design changes will make many components obsolete and require large amounts of rework.
* All records have significant errors someplace.
* Overloads will follow underloads on critical machines.
* Machines and equipment will fail when needed most.
* Tooling will break on urgent work.
* Scrap and rework will be unexpectedly larger at embarrassing times.
* Defective materials will be the only kind available when shipments must go out.
* Actual total demand will be much higher or lower than that forecasted.
* There will not be enough skilled workers to make the tricky items.
* Unforeseen operations will add excess costs.

The consensus of practically all people in manufacturing, until very recently, was that the problems experienced daily were inevitable and that it was necessary to learn to live with them. The real heroes were those individuals who could solve problems shortly after they arose, regardless of how they solved them. It is fundamental to a full understanding of how manufacturing can and should be controlled to realize that these "problems" are only symptoms of underlying diseases. These basic deficiencies are identified and discussed in Chapters 4, 5, and 6.

The evidence is overwhelming—manufacturing is out of control. This is as true in Japan, other Pacific Rim countries, and Europe as in the United States. The logical question, then, is, "How can some companies in these countries be so successful if they are not in control?" The answer, of course, is, "They are more in control than their competitors." They make better plans, execute them better, solve their problems more quickly, respond faster to needed changes, have better teamwork among their people and work more closely with suppliers and customers.

Perhaps they are luckier, although Lady Luck seems to smile more on those in manufacturing who work smarter and harder.

COMPLEXITY EXAGGERATED

The great complexity and manifold differences among the many types of manufacturing are highly visible. The myriad details of markets, materials, methods, machines, and manual operations have overawed and overwhelmed management. The large masses of data involved in planning, operating, and controlling manufacturing are seemingly unmanageable. While these statements are true, complexity and masses of details have been greatly overemphasized as reasons for lack of tight control.

The human mind grasps quickly the signals it receives from the senses but only much later perceives the basic sources and causes of the signals and understands their implications. We were aware of many details of geography, geology, volcanoes, and earthquakes long before we understood plate tectonics. So it is now with manufacturing; we need to understand the fundamentals, the essential simplicity underlying the obvious complexity.

The technical society of the field of manufacturing planning and control, The American Production and Inventory Control Society, has focused too much on techniques and too little on principles, too much on specific case studies and too little on generic applications. Computer hardware and software firms have profited more from systems' complexity and sophistication than they would have from essential simplicity. Consultants have made their reputations and fortunes promoting their expertise and experience with a few techniques identified with their favorite acronyms. Professional educators have concentrated on intellectually challenging mathematical exercises having little or no practical application in manufacturing.

Every company is unique. Some of its uniqueness lies in important characteristics but many differences are trivial. Too little work has been done to understand the total process of manufacturing and its control so that important factors are clearly distinguished from trivial. The logic and principles in this book are applicable to all; they are universal.

THE ESSENCE OF MANUFACTURING

Underlying all of the evident complexity and the apparent uniqueness of manufacturing operations is an elegant simplicity, a universal logic and some fundamental principles. The key to understanding how manufacturing works and how to control it is the perception that it involves two major flows, materials and information. These are common to manufacturing operations everywhere. They are represented by the arrows in Figure 1–1. Each will be discussed in more detail in Chapter 3.

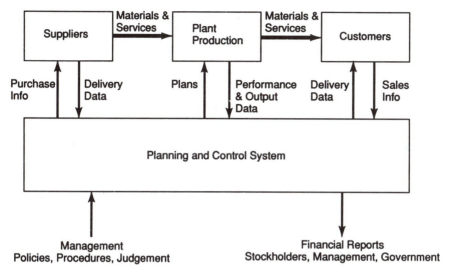

Figure 1-1   Essence of Manufacturing

Materials flow from suppliers through manufacturing plants to customers. Commonly viewed as independent organizations, the three are mutually dependent and must be considered as part of a unified process converting materials to higher value uses.

Information flows between and within the three organizations. Figure 1–1 shows four closed-loop information flows, one serving each of the three entities and one linking the system to management and providing information to outsiders, all integrated within a common business system. In directing the business, management provides input on desired policies and procedures and exercises judgment in making decisions about operations. The system produces output reports showing operating performance. It also generates reports of financial results used by management, owners, and government.

With the single-mindedness of fanatics, people in and around manufacturing focus on the bits and pieces. Customers want the right products, production workers want to know which are the right work orders, purchasing people want to get the right materials, suppliers ask which are the right orders to deliver, and managers demand the right reports. Like all fanatics, they redouble their efforts when all hope of achieving their objective is lost. There is a right way to run manufacturing to satisfy all these needs, but it is a macro, not a micro approach.

Except in continuous processing plants (refineries, food processing, and chemicals) and mass production of consumer products, the importance of flow of materials and information is largely ignored. It is ironic that terms implying motion like work-in-process (the British call it work-in-progress) and goods-in-transit are used to describe   whole classes of materials. The great bulk of such materials are not being processed, not progressing and not transitting; *they are sitting idle*.

Figure 1–2 indicates the enormous difference between the speeds of movement of information and materials. While the former can be processed at lightning speeds, the latter sit for long periods and only occasionally lurch into brief motion like the massive ice fields called glaciers.

Information moves at lightning speeds, however, only when it is being handled in machines. Telephones, facsimile machines, computers,

Figure 1–2 Information vs. Material Speeds

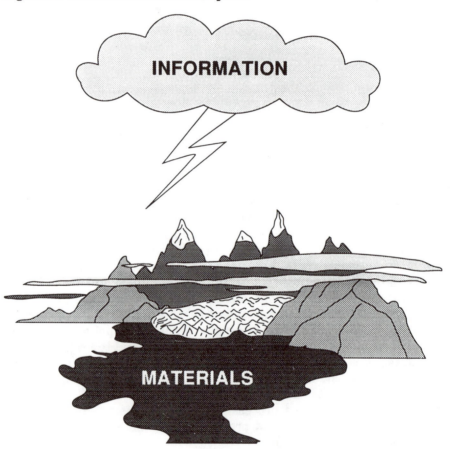

and radios transmit data, language, and pictures at the speed of light. When people get involved in information processing, the rates drop from millions of bytes in nanoseconds to a few pages a day or week. Like materials, information is stagnant over most of its useful life.

The concept of the two flows focuses attention on the need for integration of the efforts of all groups; teamwork is essential to keeping things and data moving. The activities of each organizational group influence one or both of material or information flows and must be managed to accomplish these fundamental objectives:

* Smoothing the flow
* Speeding it up
* Eliminating all waste in the total business process
* Reducing the costs of all activities

If reducing costs in one department makes flow more erratic, slows it down, or causes waste in another, it is counterproductive and undesirable. Real progress in this integration blurs the lines between organizational groups rather than clarifying them. The arm and shoulder are parts of the same body but defining where one ends and the other begins is academic; what is important is that they do well individually and together whatever the total body requires of them.

MATERIAL FLOW

Every manufacturing company procures materials and services from suppliers, processes materials to make something of higher value and provides products and/or services to customers. *It is the flow of these materials and products which is critical to the success of the business*, far more so than the materials used, the types of processes employed, the varieties of products made or the customers served.

The clearest indication of inefficiencies and ineptitude in the management of manufacturing firms is in the amount of materials lying dormant and ignored in every stage of the manufacturing process. The amount of these excesses measures the potential for improvements in operations. Henry Ford recognized this in the early 1900s; in his classic book, *Today and Tomorrow* (Bibl. 6), he said, "The thing is to keep everything in motion..." Very significant improvements in all measures of performance result when the flow of materials is speeded up.

The proportion of idle materials to total inventory varies widely among different types of manufacturing. Firms in the process industry (petroleum refineries, chemical plants, and food processors, for example) have ratios in the 10–25% range, high-volume repetitive manufacturers (consumer toiletries, hand tools, and inexpensive clothing) have 25–50% idle and batch producers (heavy machinery, airplanes and electromechanical equipment) have 95% or more of their materials sitting untouched.

The causes of idle materials are clear:

* Invalid planning, the result of excessive cycle times and record errors
* Batch sizes larger than immediate needs
* Unbalanced production operations
* Quality problems
* Design deficiencies
* "Cushions" to cope with interruptions in supply or variations in demand

None of these is easy to reduce; many believe that they are an unavoidable part of the manufacturing environment. This is not true. Experience shows that all can be attacked successfully in any manufacturing company. In fact, quick demise is the fate awaiting any firm whose competitors solve these problems and speed up material flow before it does.

INFORMATION FLOW

The flow of information is not as simple as material flow. It occurs through four closed loops as shown in Figure 1–1:

* To and from suppliers
* Within the company's operations
* To and from customers
* Between management and the company

As shown in the figure, these four flows are coordinated in and by the integrated planning and control system. In even very small companies, the amount of data to be stored and processed is so enormous that modern computers are required. Chapter 5 presents ways to apply computers to this task more effectively.

Probably the most important of all the principles applicable to manufacturing is

1. Time is the most precious resource.

Waste of time is the most heinous crime in manufacturing. Of all resources used, it is the only one which cannot be stored or replaced. It moves inexorably forward; once gone, it cannot be recovered. It is available to everyone but belongs to no one. Having the same amount of time is the only way in which humans are truly equal. Fortunately, time wasted in the past does not handicap efforts to waste less in the future.

To make better use of this priceless resource, managers can

* Be completely intolerable of the time activities are currently taking.
* Not accept as inevitable any causes of delay.
* Reject all reasons for cushions of time or inventory.
* Make reduction in cycle times of all functions a major objective in budgets, action plans, and rewards for people performing these functions.
* Set the highest priority on each group's taking less time for its work—changing what they do, not just doing it faster.

The following principle is axiomatic in all manufacturing:

2. The logic of manufacturing planning and control is simple and universal.

This logic is illustrated best in a series of questions:

* What products are to be manufactured or what services rendered?
* How many are needed?
* When are they needed?
* What resources are required?
* Which of these are available now?
* How many of the others have already been ordered?
* What more is needed and when?

These questions relate directly to the flow of materials from suppliers through manufacturing companies to customers. Chapter 4 describes how the first is answered by strategic, business, and production planning and how answers to the second and third come from master production schedules. Product bills of material, specifications, processing data, and cost information provide answers to the fourth question. The fifth question is answered by records of inventory, tooling, machinery, workers, and money, and the sixth by procurement orders for purchased raw materials, machinery, and manufactured components and by requisitions for additional workers of specified skills.

The answer to the last question is the difference between the total resources needed and those available now or being acquired soon. Obviously, these questions are appropriate for any business regardless of products, processes or materials. They apply equally well to many distribution and service firms (e.g., trucking, warehousing, banking, and airlines).

PLANNING AND CONTROL SYSTEMS

Figure 1–1 emphasizes the role of the system—coordinating all information relating to the flow of materials and operations of the company. Although separate and distinct loops are shown for suppliers, company, customers, and management, these all feed data to and extract data from the integrated system.

A cardinal principle of planning and control is

3. There is one system framework common to all types of manufacturing.

The structure of the planning and control system is common in all types of manufacturing in spite of the large number and varieties of manufacturing companies and their numerous internal differences. The individual elements making up this system are identified and discussed in detail in Chapter 5 and the truth of this principle is demonstrated there.

There is no inherent need in any manufacturing company for several separate systems having duplicate data files, redundant techniques, or different software logic to process the requisite information. In fact, this approach will preclude tight control. The reasons for this are presented in Chapter 5.

At first glance, the next principle may seem contradictory:

4. There is no one best way to control manufacturing.

A good analogy is the family car. Several families may have the same automobile but use it in widely different ways—going shopping, commuting, taking children to school, or touring. Parts of the vehicle are of different interest to the various members of the family—instruments on the dashboard to Dad, contents of the glovebox to Mom, stereo tape player to the children.

Likewise, the planning and control system, identical in its basic framework for all companies, is useful in helping each company achieve its objectives—rapid growth, increased market share, introduction of new products—however different these may be from the objectives of other firms. The system is also a help to the individual parts of a company's organization regardless of how different their needs may be.

Although the system framework is common to all, specific elements may be of greater or lesser importance in one company than in another. Forecasting is a minor or negligible activity in aerospace and defense firms, for example, and capacity planning and control in the process industry is part of plant design, not operations. The foregoing principle emphasizes that *the way the system is used may be as different as the companies using it*. Many executives, managers and "experts" in manufacturing control have not seen this distinction clearly. The result has been an unnecessary proliferation of different, overly complex systems.

Planning is the activity of assigning numbers to future activities. Execution is converting plans into reality. Control is achieved by comparing execution to plans, detecting significant deviations, reporting them to the proper persons and taking prompt corrective actions. Computer-based systems are planning and control devices; people execute.

Planning, execution, and control are separate and distinct activities and must be viewed and understood individually. They must be tightly integrated, however; this is the most important role of the system. This is covered in detail in Chapter 6.

IMPROVING FLEXIBILITY

"The only thing constant is change" has never been more true. Now the rate of change increases constantly—products live shorter lives, new materials appear more frequently, new process technologies are developed more often and new market opportunities arise almost every week. Anyone who doesn't enjoy fast-paced change will be very unhappy in manufacturing.

The resources used in manufacturing have greater or lesser degrees of flexibility. Time, people, and money are the most adaptable to a wide variety of uses but plants, suppliers, machinery, tooling, raw materials, and common components can also be used to produce different items. Preserving this flexibility is essential to responding rapidly and correctly to change.

A very important principle of manufacturing, providing a basic strategy of operations, is

5. Do not commit flexible resources to any specific item until the last possible moment.

Chapter 4 relates the validity of a plan inversely to the time horizon over which it extends; committing flexible resources before it is absolutely necessary to do so links execution to plans of very suspect reliability. It gives customers more time to change their minds about how many of what products they want by which date, design engineers have more opportunity to redesign items actually being worked on, and specific products are made long before they are really needed.

This problem has been most acute in aerospace, defense, and heavy equipment businesses where progress payments by customers have made the cost of capital tied up in inventory a negligible factor in management thinking. Such payments have even been viewed as beneficial in improving cash flow. Few executives and managers in such firms really know that *only a few hours or, at most, a few days of work are required to produce the materials their companies buy and to make the products they build*. They accept without question the idea that planned lead times must be weeks, months, or even years. Coupled with strong but mistaken convictions that contracts, and the plans based on them, are firm and that starting work earlier will improve chances of finishing on time, aerospace, defense, and heavy equipment makers begin execution months too early.

Cutting to an irreducible minimum the time between starting and finishing production, thereby delaying the use of resources until the latest moment, requires critical attention to every activity contributing to production cycle times. Figure 1–3 shows the two-pronged attack needed. Using the priority side of the planning and control system, action can be taken to reduce the variance in lead time by straightening flow paths and tightening priority control. The capacity side of the system is used to reduce the length of the lead time by shortening and

Figure 1–3 Production Cycle Management

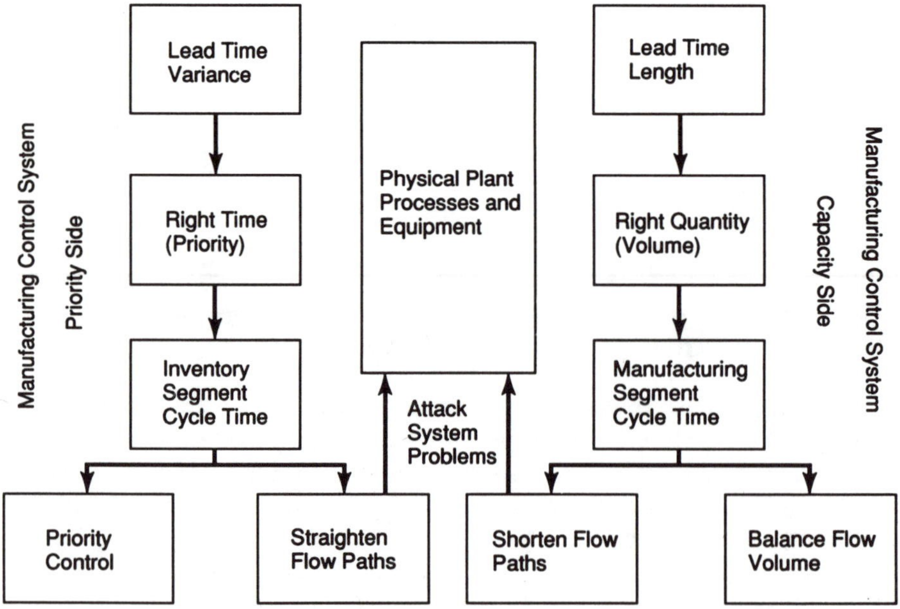

smoothing out material flow paths. Both types of actions reduce the amount of materials sitting in inventory in storehouses, work-in-process or other queues. Note that Figure 1–3 also states "Attack system problems"; this is needed to reduce material delays caused by holdups in information flow.

The technical changes needed to reduce queues of work, setup times, processing times, and move times are easily made. Convincing people that this must be done, however, is very difficult. Before they will attack excessive cushions of time and materials, people must accept some very important conceptual changes. Many believe these cushions are absolutely necessary to cope with uncertainties and upsets so frequent in manufacturing. Few believe that the causes of the uncertainties and upsets can be attacked successfully.

The five principles discussed in this chapter are universal. They can and must be applied in every manufacturing business. The benefits are evident in the success of a rapidly growing number of firms. Failure to apply them is equally visible in companies in great difficulty and those which have gone under.

THEORY AND PRACTICE

The first law of manufacturing developed in this book can be stated simply:

In manufacturing operations, all benefits will be directly proportional to the speed of flow of materials and information.

It is easy to say, as this law does, what must be done to achieve excellence in operations and world-class competitive stature. No one will quarrel with the desirability of smoothing out and speeding up the flows of materials and information. Serious problems arise, however, when details of how to do this are considered. This book presents tested and proven approaches which support the theory and illustrate how any manufacturing business can greatly improve operations.

There are four important corollaries of this theory:

Corollary 1—This law applies to every type of manufacturing business.

Corollary 2—The tightness of control of manufacturing activities will vary inversely with their cycle times.

Corollary 3—Any planning and control system will be more effective with fewer problems causing slower flow rates of materials and information.

Corollary 4—Solving one problem which slows down or interrupts material or information flow will cost less and be more effective than efforts to cope with the problem's effects.

The validity of each of these corollaries will be demonstrated in the following chapters of this book.

As stated at the beginning of this chapter, theory alone is impotent; it must be supported by actions. Actions, however vigorously taken and energetically continued, must be consistent with theory or they will be futile at best and fatal at worst. Lacking knowledge of manufacturing theory and confused by its complexity, executives and managers looking for quick fixes embark enthusiastically on highly touted programs and are frustrated by failure.

Business Week, in its January 20, 1986 cover story, "Business Fads: What's In—and Out," reviewed four decades of fads, listing a total of 20 ideas that were popular with management. How many can you remember? How many can you still define? How many did your company try out? How well did they work?

> 1950s—Computerization, Theory X, Quantitative Management, Diversification, and Management by Objectives.
>
> 1960s—T-Groups, Centralization/Decentralization, Matrix Management, Conglomeration, and the Management Grid.
>
> 1970s—Zero-based Budgeting, Experience Curve, and Portfolio Management.
>
> 1980s—Theory Z, Intrapreneuring, Demassing, Restructuring, Corporate Culture, One-Minute Managing, and Management by Walking Around.

Business Week commented that "...a lot of American executives these days seem eager to latch on to almost any new concept that promises a quick fix for their problems." The article also stated that, "There's nothing inherently wrong with any of these ideas. What's wrong is that too many companies use them as gimmicks to evade the basic challenges they face." Amen! Managers who don't really know how manufacturing can and should be run are frequently mislead by fine-sounding concepts that promise quick and easy cures for serious problems which they don't know how to solve.

The consensus of most executives directing manufacturing firms is that planning, control, and execution of production are highly detailed, very technical, mathematical, computer-based activities in which their staff specialists often perform poorly. The managers responsible for planning and control find their efforts thwarted by their peers in other departments. These, in turn, resist valiantly all attempts by others to interfere in their spheres of authority and are frustrated by what they see as poor planning and control.

Compartmentalized organization, pride in and protection of specialist status, technical jargon, and the lack of cross-training of people in key roles in the organization has hindered the development of the necessary understanding of mutual interests among these people. Awareness of common interests and development of teamwork among all functions in the organization are prerequisites for success. All must understand the first law.

Peters and Waterman in their widely acclaimed book, *In Search of Excellence* (Bibl. 13) identified eight attributes of excellent and innovative companies:

1. A bias for action
2. Close to the customer
3. Autonomy and entrepreneurship
4. Productivity through people
5. Hands on, value driven
6. Stick to the knitting
7. Simple form, lean staff
8. Simultaneous loose-tight properties

These were really strategies and policies followed by the companies used as examples and rated successful. They were intended to show management *what to do to* be as successful. Managers need to know also *how to do it* and *why it works*; these were not fully explained by Peters and Waterman.

Another popular book, Richard Schonberger's *Japanese Manufacturing Techniques* (Bibl. 24) presented nine lessons to be learned from the Japanese:

1. Management technology is a highly transportable commodity.
2. Just-in-time production exposes problems otherwise hidden by excess inventories and staff.
3. Quality begins with production and requires a companywide "habit of improvement."
4. Culture is no obstacle; (just-in-time) techniques can change behavior.
5. Simplify (plant layout), and goods will flow like water.
6. Flexibility (in production-line management) opens doors.
7. Travel light and make numerous trips (in purchasing)—like the water beetle.
8. More self-improvement, fewer programs, less specialist intervention (in worker development).
9. Simplicity is the natural state.

This book, described on the dust jacket as a handbook, tells middle managers *how to* apply these nine lessons. The book calls them "hidden lessons," without explaining why, and refers to their "inherent good sense," implying that they should be obvious. Perhaps the purloined letter syndrome is working here; valuable things being sought are right in front of the people seeking them but are overlooked. This sometimes happens in manufacturing.

More often, however, the lessons are seen, even understood, but are deemed inapplicable. This was the reaction of many executives to my Special Roundtable Report (Bibl. 17) on just-in-time practices in many successful companies; their first comments were on the differences between their operations and the case companies. Experts baldly stating that successful practices are transferable from Japanese to U.S. companies have not convinced managers who lack understanding of the theory and principles. Lack of such knowledge hamstrings effective action.

Another important factor in motivating managers to improve their operations is that the right actions are so often counterintuitive. Many managers base decisions on conventional wisdom, particularly in activities where they lack real experience or sound understanding. Without a sound understanding of theory, they follow common practice, often exactly the wrong thing to do. Some examples are given and debunked in Chapter 2. Such common sense is no help; real understanding is too uncommon.

Harold Geneen's fine book *Managing* (Bibl. 7) stresses the profound truth of the simple statement, "Management must manage." By his definitions, management is the team of managers who operate a business and managing means getting things done. The word "must" between "management" and "managing" places full responsibility on managers when failures to execute plans occur as well as when poor plans are made; blaming others is no excuse. Geneen understood that managing is more than making good plans and trying hard to implement them; it is making them happen, executing them successfully.

"Decide what it is you want to do, and then start doing it" was Geneen's philosophy; he saw clearly the need for fast action. He knew also the importance of fast flow and low inventories. Cycle times and inventory turnover were topics of almost every management meeting he conducted. He used these meetings to bring out division problems and to apply the vast experience of the group to getting fast solutions. He understood manufacturing; his record of 14 years of higher profits every quarter for ITT's diverse operations shows how well he understood it.

Other experts—economists, consultants, educators, and political leaders—waxed eloquent during the 1970s and 1980s interpreting the statistical signs which told the state of U.S. manufacturing and foretold its future. Their analyses and prognoses were as inconsistent and unreliable as the dire warnings of the sages of old using chicken entrails. From their mouthings came such pessimistic terms as "sunset industries" and "postindustrial economy"; optimism was expressed in terms like "high tech" and "service." Extrapolating statistics is deadly—to the extrapolator. Underlying all statistics-based projections is the assumption that the future will be like the past. The presumption of no changes in the environment is the fallacy.

Instead of the inevitability of current trends projected into the future, the theme of this book is that knowledgeable managers can and will bring about the changes necessary to ensure a sound, healthy, growing industrial economy in the United States. The ingredients are available; knowledge and motivation must come so that the corrective actions are taken in time. The prerequisites for making it happen are

* All executives committed to its successful implementation
* A complete, integrated, computer-based business system used by all needing data and information
* A very high level of data integrity
* Qualified people throughout the organization with continuing education to become more competent
* Refusal to accept any problem as unsolvable
* A high energy level to innovate
* Patience to tolerate mistakes combined with unrelenting determination to succeed

Of these prerequisites, the most important is education of executives and managers to develop their full understanding of how manufacturing really works and how it should be managed. It is also the most difficult task required; all technical and operational problems are easier to solve quickly.

The implementation of the first law in successful companies is characterized by

* Employing the talents of all people to improve operations
* Viewing each activity as part of the total customer-company-supplier network
* Improving quality of output of all activities
* Designing products for manufacturability
* Ensuring adequate capacity to process all materials and information
* Smoothing out and speeding up material and information flows
* Increasing flexibility and speed of response to changes
* Increasing productivity of all activities
* Identifying problems quickly and fixing them fast
* Employing simple, pertinent measures of performance

Any company can develop these characteristics given the will to do it and the leadership of qualified executives. It is not easy to do. It's a new way of life to most people in most firms.

Success in achieving it will be indicated by

* Constant improvement in all important performance measures
* Very high customer satisfaction
* Support by loyal suppliers
* Increased stability of employment
* Stronger competitive position
* Fewer crises and faster responses
* A guaranteed future

The first law of manufacturing presented in this chapter is a concise statement defining the fundamentals by which manufacturing businesses should be run. It applies to all types of manufacturing processes, all industries and all companies in any free-market country. Don't be misled by the word "theory"; everything presented in this book has been tested and proven in practice.

Chapter 2 provides perspective on recent developments and distinguishes some facts from fables. Chapter 3 looks at the total process called manufacturing in detail and highlights the flows of material and information. Chapter 4 presents the planning hierarchy every business needs and defines managements' roles in this part of the process. Chapter 5 shows the elements of systems and their role in controlling all operations and activities. Chapter 6 describes how operations can be planned and controlled effectively. Chapter 7 shows how conventional accounting practices can mislead management, defines important measures of performance, reasonable tolerances, and measurement points; and identifies sources of data, ways to determine data reliability, and the effects of errors. Chapter 8 presents some fallacies which must be unlearned and some strategies for success in the future.

Included throughout are basic principles and practical techniques and their application. The language is nontechnical, business English, concise for busy managers. Supporting details of a mathematical, statistical, and technical nature are referenced in the bibliography for those interested in more in-depth knowledge. The objective is easy reading for busy people who seek the knowledge of how to improve manufacturing.

CHAPTER 2

Evolution, Facts, and Fables

The most sophisticated statistics on the most powerful computer will not accomplish as much as elimination of one cause of chaos.

SUMMARY

Most manufacturing firms now face global competition for global markets. Many theories (and solutions) have been proposed to explain (and reverse) shrinking U.S. economic power. The principal causes are handicaps of government, union, and financial groups, foreign market constraints; scarce and expensive capital; and poor management.

Three ways exist to generate wealth: manufacturing, agriculture, and extraction. Some service activities assist these wealth generators but most simply redistribute it after middlemen slice off a significant share. Prior to the 1970s, America led the world in the production of goods and in productivity. During these years, management changed from production experts to marketing and then to financial specialists.

During the 1970s, the structure, principles, and techniques of production planning and control were developed, making tight control possible. However, expensive systems implemented with great effort in many companies fell far short of expectations.

By the 1980s, the importance of short lead times, flexibility and solving seemingly inevitable problems was recognized. In this decade, however, many more U.S. firms lost competitiveness, and even powerful defense contractors found themselves in trouble. A firm's inventory measures the degree of its control but few top-level managers understand what causes it or how to control it. Too few also realize that tinkering with planned lead times adds to their problems and aggravates business cycles.

At the end of the 1980s, manufacturing in the United States reached a critical stage. Formal, computer-based planning and control systems were oversold, and underused. They are not panaceas and, too often, are fragmented, incomplete, or overly sophisticated. Tight control does not require complex systems. Another myth accepted by nonmanufacturing managers is that ability to "read the numbers" is sufficient to run manufacturing companies well. Mergers, acquisitions, hostile takeovers, leveraged buyouts, and other financial manipulations have been a major factor in the decline of U.S. industry. Qualified, educated management knows how manufacturing can and must be run. It is not too late to reverse the trend and return American industry to competitiveness in world markets.

DECLINE OF U.S. MANUFACTURING

With only rare exceptions, manufacturing companies in every country now find themselves with competitors in other nations for global markets. Over four decades of general world peace, the perfection of instantaneous communication, and the establishment of worldwide markets have made information on technological developments available to practically anyone anywhere. Fast, economical transportation of people and materials makes closeness to sources and markets a minor factor. Since the mid-1960s, U.S. manufacturing companies have been losing competitive battles with foreign companies at an accelerating rate. A short list of the industries essentially lost to foreign competition, principally Japan, includes

Radios	Television sets	Tape recorders
VCRs	Small appliances	Power tools
Binoculars	Cameras	Telescopes
Watches	Clocks	Timers
Textiles	Shoes	Hats
Bicycles	Motorcycles	Snowmobiles
Trucks	Ships	Machine tools
Steel	Castings	Small hardware

The U.S. won the war against Japan, but Japan is obviously and decisively winning the peaceful exploitation of U.S. markets.

Many theories are advanced to account for the dwindling economic power of the United States. Each is accompanied by a proposed solution, usually requiring some group other than the proponent's to straighten itself out. Unfair competition is charged, including trade restrictions, dumping, and stealing of secrets; these accusations support claims for protection by U.S. tariffs and other free trade restrictions. Those making such claims include executives in threatened firms and labor leaders fearing loss of union jobs. They, and all opponents of free trade, prefer to ignore the fundamental truth that protection of one industry in today's integrated economies will be at the expense of everyone using the products; tariffs protect producers at the expense of consumers.

Many others ascribe the cause to differentials in the wages of workers in industrial and developing countries, accepting the demise of sunset and smokestack industries in the United States as inevitable. These ignore the other important factors in the total cost equation—productivity; quality; distance-related expenses; inventory investment; and flexibility to respond to market, product, and process changes. As in most similar ill-considered analyses of causes and recommended solutions, the cure would be worse than the disease.

There are four principal causes of the decline in American industrial power. Not in order of importance, they are

* Operating under governmental, labor union, and financial institution handicaps competitors do not have.
* Trading in markets with very different rules.
* Scarce and expensive capital.
* Poor management.

America's competition has benefited significantly from supportive government, cooperative unions, less financial pressure, cheaper and more plentiful capital, open markets, and favorable trade relations. Without their handicaps, American managers also would perform far better.

Governmental Handicaps

Relations between U.S. industry and government have been characterized by antagonism at worst and benign neglect at best. Preoccupied with diplomatic and military matters abroad and social programs at home, government has tinkered with financial manipulations to steer the economy but has shied away from developing an industrial policy to ensure a sound economy. Separation of business and government seems to be almost as rigid as separation of church and state.

Political leaders operate on an apparent assumption that free trade and the historical strength of the American economy will provide both the money and muscle needed for leadership of the free world and the wealth to afford domestic social programs. Although it is now obvious to many others, politicians seem not to have realized that U.S. world leadership and domestic programs are both being undermined by a faltering economy.

Union Handicaps

Abetted by favorable laws, labor unions have long maintained an aggressive, antagonistic approach to relations with management. In the steadily worsening economic climate of the 1980s in manufacturing, many progressive labor leaders saw the need for cooperating with management to ensure the survival of companies facing strong competition. Most reverted to old attitudes when profits returned. Some have not yet awakened to reality. Few foreign competitors have this problem.

Financial Institution Handicaps

Unrestrained manipulations of manufacturing companies' finances, begun in the 1970s, has been a significant factor in the loss of competitive position by American corporations. Hostile takeovers, ill-considered acquisitions, indiscriminate mergers, and other financial manipulations have diverted into the pockets of lawyers and financiers millions in capital which could have been used for improving manufacturing and increasing the nation's real wealth. Their avowed purpose—to improve the shareholders' stake—ignores the interests of employees, suppliers, customers, and the general public, all of whom deserve consideration also.

Defending against possible takeovers by raiders generates an obsession to improve stock values and to inordinately high pressures to maintain and enhance short-term earnings. These have distracted managers from long-term objectives and reduced investment in research and development of new processes and products. In its January 8, 1987 issue, *The Wall Street Journal*, in a column titled "Myopic Managers?" concluded that "U.S. companies are damaging their future vitality, and even viability, through reluctance to undertake long-term investments and new product development. Some see this myopia threatening the nation's economic growth."

In his book, *The Reckoning* (Bibl. 9), David Halberstam associated the beginnings of American automakers' problems with the postwar emergence of financial specialists as a major force in the industry. These people are rarely saboteurs; they are often megalomaniacs and sometimes greedy, but many believe sincerely that they are promoting the best interests of the corporation. However, their lack of understanding of manufacturing, coupled with use of the wrong performance measures as described in Chapter 7, causes their activities to be very destructive of sound performance.

Trade Relations

Trade negotiations carried on over many years between Japan and the U.S. have been characterized by a succession of increasingly bitter claims. Americans accused Japan of unfair practices, and Japanese cried that they were misunderstood; both were right. American goods and services met strong, effective opposition in Japanese markets, while U.S. markets were open to Japanese products. The Japanese, intent on building a powerful economic base at home, did not believe their practices "unfair." In spite of "concessions" by the Japanese, only token penetration of their markets has been achieved by U.S. firms, even those making serious efforts. Technologies developed at great effort and cost in the U.S. continue to be transferred to Japan at very little cost. The reasons for these practices and the actions required to reverse them are complex and are beyond the scope of this book. Excellent coverage is found in Clyde Prestowitz' *Trading Places* (Bibl.   23).

Poor Management

The manufacturing environment changed very dramatically and the technology of planning and control was revolutionized in the 1970s and 1980s. Too many managers have failed to realize that either change has occurred and very few understand the implications.

Only a few top-level executives in U.S. manufacturing firms have had any significant amount of experience in production operations; most have risen through the ranks of finance, sales, and marketing. The prestigious business schools develop MBA candidates holding the conviction that they need to know only "how to read the numbers" to manage any type of company. This is a deadly fallacy. It is equally fallacious, however, to believe that top managers need in-depth knowledge of production details, requiring weeks of time and study of masses of technical details.

Executives in manufacturing companies need to understand the fundamentals of how manufacturing really works and how it can be planned and controlled effectively. Unfortunately, most of them do not know that their understanding is deficient and see no need to exert themselves to learn. They do not know what they don't know and don't want to find out. Getting their attention to learning and applying new knowledge in this field is a very challenging undertaking.

Of the four major causes of decline in U.S. industry, poor management is the one meriting an all-out attack because

* Management attitudes can be changed quickly (witness their response to just-in-time and total quality control).

* The changes are mainly internal to individual firms.
* Very significant benefits will come fast.

WEALTH GENERATION AND SHARING

A sound economy in any country is dependent on healthy, growing wealth generation. There are only three ways to create wealth—agriculture (growing grains, vegetables, fruit, and animals), extraction (separating valuable minerals and liquids from the earth and seas), and manufacturing (converting low-value materials to higher-value products). All other activities of government, the professions (medicine, law, and dentistry) and the so-called "service" industries (banking, insurance, personal services, communications, and transportation), simply redistribute the wealth generated by these three. In the United States, all wealth generators have been in trouble.

The importance of manufacturing as a wealth generator should be obvious. By converting low-value materials into higher-value products, companies contribute directly to increasing the standard of living of all people in the countries in which they operate as well as those from which they procure goods and services.

Some service activities assist the wealth generators. These include banking, insurance, and transportation; they make some contribution to a society's standard of living. Most make very little such contribution, however, and are mainly redistributors of wealth. They provide employment and useful services, but they generate no real wealth. The service activities' dependence on manufacturing, agriculture, and extraction is seen clearly by the way they thrive or suffer with the true wealth generators in periodic boom-and-bust business cycles.

Many seem to think that service industries (the information society, for example) will make up the future economy of the United States. They have provided jobs for a large portion of a growing labor force but at much lower wages and salaries than manufacturing. In addition, their people's productivity is very low and improving only very slowly. In their interesting book, *Service Operations Management* (Bibl. 5), Fitzsimmons and Sullivan provide an in-depth comparison of service operations and manufacturing, highlighting many other factors.

The concept that manufacturing could be allowed to die and could be replaced by service work received wide publicity and acceptance. This is a fallacy; the United States needs both. The real tragedy in these service developments is that their glamour detracted attention from solving the problems in manufacturing and diverted intelligent people from industry. Since service industries do not generate real wealth, however, it is obvious that they cannot be depended upon in the long term to support a rising (or even a constant) standard of living for the growing population of the United States.

The idea that the United States, or any other major industrial nation, can support a growing population and maintain or improve its standard of living via an "information-based economy" is misleading fiction, to give it the best possible interpretation.

In America, industry has had bad press. The media and the educators see and tell little good about manufacturing. Common terms like "the rat race," "exploitation of labor," "dog eat dog," and "business is business" connote heartlessness, greed, and lack of scruples. Profit is a dirty word and is commonly believed to be exorbitant. Industry is accused of false advertising, willfully polluting the environment, cheating customers, and endangering the lives and health of workers and others. Its role in generating wealth is largely ignored. Very few bright young people see their future in manufacturing.

The wealth manufacturing creates is shared among employees (wages, salaries, and bonuses), managers (salaries and bonuses), owners (stock dividends and capital appreciation), government (taxes), and suppliers of goods and services (prices). The shares of wealth among workers, managers, and owners are determined by a multitude of factors—stock prices, strength of unions, availability of skilled people, special skills, unusual abilities, and business cycles are a few. Enough has been written on this; it will not be discussed in this book.

Governments' shares, taxes, are established by legislators (usually lawyers) making unilateral decisions. Those who make such decisions, unfortunately, have little understanding of and less consideration for the possible damaging effects of excessive taxes and regulations on wealth-generation processes. It is ironic that those communities without industry attempt to attract it by offering low-tax incentives while those with it look on it as a limitless source of higher revenues. The lessons of recent economic history in America and the underlying causes of Eastern Europe's stunning political changes seem lost in too narrowly focused publicity on unpopular political leaders and very popular ideals of freedom.

Suppliers of materials and services get their shares of real wealth from the prices they charge. Arm's-length, antagonistic relations between suppliers and customers are giving way to more cooperative "partnerships" in which both share all relevant information, work closely together, and also share the benefits. This is the trend of the future.

In our complex economy, we have found millions of ways in which people can "make money," meaning earn income. The ultimate source of such money is a wealth generator and there are only three types of these. All else is redistribution of wealth, with high prices paid to the middlemen.

THE EVOLUTION OF PLANNING AND CONTROL

The "science" of manufacturing planning and control has been evolving over the last century. Figure 2–1 lists some of the more important events in that evolution which began in the 1880s with the studies of Frederick Taylor, Frank and Lillian Gilbreth, Harrington Emerson, Henry Gantt, and other engineers on how to increase the efficiency of human labor in industry.

Figure 2–1 Evolution of Planning and Control

1882 - 1912	Scientific Management Developed
1915	Economic Order Quality Formula Published
1934	Statistical Order Points Proposed
1957	American Production and Inventory Control Society (APICS) Organized
1960	Business Computer Hardware and Software Introduced
1960s	Material Requirements Planning Applied
1972	APICS Certification Program Started
	Body of Knowledge and Language Codified
	Principles and Techniques Defined
1973	Integrated Manufacturing Systems Applied
1980s	Global Competition Intensified

During and immediately after World War II practically every major manufacturing company in the United States was directed by managers who understood the manufacturing process. Our role as "the arsenal of democracy" was well earned in the prodigious output of airplanes, ships, guns, and other wartime materials.The morale and work ethics of American workers was very high, labor unions were not antagonistic and made little selfish use of their power and government was sympathetic and cooperative in assisting manufacturing in meeting the needs of the country and its allies.

America's industrial machine, unlike that of all other industrial countries, was unaffected by war damage. For several years, it continued to supply most of the world's needs and profited accordingly. When the war-starved consumer demand for automobiles, household appliances, and other peacetime products was satisfied in the early 1950s, the needs of industry changed from manufacturing expertise to an understanding of markets and their creation and enlargement. Managers with these skills became the driving forces in industry.

The 1960s were characterized by great growth and prosperity. U.S. workers led the industrial world in productivity and American products dominated world markets. Labor unions grew in strength and influence and demanded a larger share of the pie. Government agencies no longer viewed industry as one of the major sources of real wealth but rather as sources of revenue, oppressors of labor, polluters of the environment, and threats to the health of workers and citizens. Corporate taxes became a major source of money for redistribution to those believed deserving.

Direct labor wages rose rapidly as did fringe benefits of all workers. Material costs rose steadily. The costs of safety devices to protect workers and indirect taxes for welfare and medical plans escalated; industry, however, was able to pass the bulk of these cost increases along to their customers in higher prices and felt no real pain.

In the 1960s, the reasons for the conflicts among three of the important objectives of manufacturing companies—better customer satisfaction, higher profits, and lower capital investment—became clear. They all depend on properly managed inventory and production. The basic principles and the techniques needed to resolve these conflicts were still only vaguely understood. The structure of systems within which these techniques would work together effectively had not yet been defined. Practitioners were preoccupied with a search for practical techniques and academies with elegant mathematical solutions to a few minor problems. Undoubtedly, the derivation of the formula for calculating an "economic order quantity," published by Ford Harris in 1915 in *Operations and Costs*, (Bibl. 11) was valuable in reducing costs associated with ordering batches of materials. Application of statistical analyses to setting protective levels of safety stocks, presented by R. H. Wilson in 1934 in *A Scientific Routine for Stock Control* (Bibl. 28) provided practitioners with another useful tool. During this decade, the development of the computer for business uses made available the tool needed for handling the large masses of data involved.

Enhancing these techniques by deriving more sophisticated mathematical models, however, added little value. Worse, it distracted people from thinking about the solution of the problems which made use of these techniques necessary. Top management generally ignored the whole situation.

In the 1970s, many significant changes appeared. Managers with financial acumen saw benefits to their companies (and to themselves) in mergers and acquisitions and the craze to develop conglomerates became the obsession of many top-level managers. Such managers had little understanding of manufacturing and how it should be operated and viewed companies like stocks and bonds in a portfolio to be manipulated for the maximum financial return to the conglomerate. Manufacturing managers who knew how operations should be run were now second-class citizens in the management hierarchy.

During this decade, the term "postindustrial society" was used to describe the economy of the United States. Daniel Bell's *"Five Dimensions of Post-Industrial Society"* (Bibl. 1) identified five characteristics of this type of economy as

1. *The creation of a service economy*. High, increasing productivity in manufacturing supports the growth of services, just as improved agriculture supported manufacturing. Since the late 1970s, the number of service people employed has exceeded that in manufacturing and the percentage of gross personal consumption expenditures has exceeded those for goods.

2. *The preeminence of professional and technical people*. Service occupations require higher-level skills and education. Individuals with these expect more interesting and challenging work than is available in manufacturing.

3. *The primacy of theoretical knowledge*. Rapid growth of technology in turn demands more research and development of new materials, products and processes. Knowledge workers, as Peter Drucker calls them, find little attraction in production.

4. *The planning of technology*. Potentially dangerous side effects of new technologies—pesticides, industrial wastes, drugs, and radiation, for example—retard and may prevent their application in industry and society. Broad multidisciplined knowledge is needed for such evaluations.

5. *The rise of new intellectual technology*. Applying the power of computers to manipulate information, artificial intelligence, and other new "sciences" requires the services of people of the highest intelligence and innovative thinking.

In the 1970s, the development of manufacturing planning and control systems was progressing rapidly. The basic principles by which manufacturing should be operated were identified. The language and body of knowledge of the field were codified and certification examinations developed to identify qualified individuals. The necessary techniques for planning and control systems were developed and tested. Sound computer-based systems were installed in many progressive companies. A few outstanding companies demonstrated the validity of the principles and the effectiveness of the techniques but these unfortunately were rare exceptions. The bulk of the money and efforts spent on such installations did not generate a small fraction of the potential returns.

The greatest single reason for these failures was the perception of planning and control systems as tools of the technicians rather than as primary means for management to operate the total business. In addition, whole industries such as automotive, defense, aerospace, and machine tools saw little application to their operations of the successful approaches in repetitive and batch types of production. They saw themselves as "different" and hence in need of entirely different control approaches. While these attitudes have been changing rapidly in automotive and process industries, they changed very slowly in defense and aerospace companies. The machine tool industry is still suffering badly for its lack of attention.

In the 1960s, practitioners sought the right amount of safety stock to buffer operations against variations in demand and uncertainties of supply in an extremely hostile environment. Computers and statistical techniques were employed in futile efforts to put the right cushions in the right places at the proper time.

In the 1970s, computers and MRP systems were employed to provide more accurate dates on schedules so that the proper priorities could be used to improve performance. These focused some managers on the need for accurate data, valid master plans, and the value of sound execution. Too many still have not learned these lessons.

In the 1980s, the importance of short lead times and flexibility and the practability of solving many of the problems of manufacturing became clear. Terms like stockless production and just-in-time were the popular buzzwords, causing flurries of activity in many companies but producing dramatic improvements in only a few. This was not because the concepts which the terms embodied were fallacious. Too many managers did not make the effort to understand the prerequisites. Some hoped instead for some "magic." Some avoided the work required with excuses that the ideas were limited in application to high-volume producers or that they required big investments to cut lot-sizes and alter plant layout. Such excuses, all erroneous, showed their basic ignorance in this important arena of manufacturing businesses.

Educational programs for practitioners proliferated in colleges, universities, and computer hardware and software companies, and a full spectrum was offered by technical societies and consultants. While such courses were available to executives, few attended. Company budgets contained significant sums for training workers and staff people. Professionals could be identified by certification. Technical societies for different disciplines like purchasing, quality assurance, and planning and control began to work together.

The 1980s found many U.S. manufacturing companies in very serious trouble. Few had customers satisfied with their product quality, on-time deliveries, and flexibility for change. Most had much more capital tied up in inventory than they wanted. The old approaches to profit improvement using marketing promotions and direct labor incentives were ineffective and capital was not available for the automation they believed necessary for higher productivity. Competitors were eating them up.

The situation in aerospace and defense companies was even more acutely embarrassing. The Defense Contract Audit Agency had found serious discrepancies between actual charges to the U.S. government and those they deemed justified. These were somehow associated with "MRP systems." The advantages of using the MRP technique to combine requirements for items common to several products or programs are obvious and significant. Most A/D companies, however, had long lead times, long-time overlapping of orders processing components for two or more contracts, frequent design changes, many quality problems, and varying priorities.

These result in multiple changes in material usage and allocations. However, progress payments and contract auditing requirements dictate detailed tracking of costs and materials allocated to specific contracts. Massive data manipulations via complex systems must be made in attempts to meet auditing requirements in such a fluid environment. The data are often incorrect and always suspect.

It was these problems that caused the debacle in 1987 in which the Defense Contract Audit Agency challenged over 300 major contractors to prove that their "MRP systems" were not causing noncompliance with contract provisions and yielding millions of dollars in illegal payments. Really ironic was the fact that few A/D companies had MRP systems, even if the term were interpreted very liberally.

The simple solution to this very serious problem is to keep to a minimum the amount of materials in the execution phase of production and also to shorten times between start and completion following principle 5 and not committing flexible resources to specific requirements until the last possible moment. The potential benefits are very large in aerospace/defense companies.

The 1980s marked the beginning of the age of maturity and sound applications. Unfortunately, success was limited to too few companies in the United States and the Western industrial world. Pacific Rim countries where the principles and techniques were strongly embraced began to dominate global competition.

INVENTORY FALLACIES AND TRUTHS

Control of total inventory is one of the most important criteria. Here manufacturing companies show most clearly when they are out of control. In such companies, inventory is viewed as an independent variable. Budgets are set by arbitrary decisions, unrelated to operating plans, often only wishful thinking that the coming year will see improvements over the past. Management expectations are low; most seem to believe that a 50% increase in inventory turnover is very ambitious. Most are satisfied with turnover rates in single digits.

Very few managers know what inventory's true role is and what makes it so unpredictable. Budgeted totals are rarely met. Many managers think inventories are subject only to Shakespeare's "slings and arrows of outrageous fortune."

While it is listed prominently among the assets, inventory is almost invariably treated as a liability. Although most managers think there is some "right" amount for their business, few know what it is or even how to find out. The consensus is that less would be better but would probably jeopardize customer service and might even cause costs to rise. Such is conventional wisdom today.

The role of inventories in the drama of business cycles has been the subject of much discussion by economists, journalists, politicians, and business leaders. These disagree on the proper actions to take to reduce the effects of surging inventories. Their statements make it obvious that few of them understand fully the relationship of inventories to production and the true causes of inventory fluctuations. Their common belief is that inventories must rise when production output grows and must fall when it drops. If this premise is accepted as true, swings in production rates will be amplified, higher production rates will be needed to meet the double impact of rising sales and larger inventories, and vice versa.

The truth, of course, is that there is no more need to change inventory levels to meet rising and falling sales rates than there is to change the depth of water in a tank to react to changes in faucet fill and drain rates. The key to keeping inventory (and water) levels where desired is balancing input with output. Varying production promptly to meet demand changes makes changes in inventory level unnecessary. When its role in production is understood and the true causes of inventory excesses and fluctuations are known and addressed, it will have much less harmful influence on business cycles.

The Paradox of Inventory Control

Inventory, its nature, and its control are possibly the least understood of all facets of manufacturing. A multitude of techniques—mathematical, physical, and computerized—are viewed by most practitioners as necessary to control it. Little is written, however, on the basic process by which inventory is really controlled. Figure 2–2 illustrates the concepts involved. "Inventory" is represented by the amount of liquid in the container; additions are called "inputs" and reductions are "outputs." Inputs include receipts of purchased and manufactured items and returns from external sources; outputs consist of issues to fabrication and assembly and shipments to external customers. Large scrap losses and record adjustments may be significant factors but their presence indicates that serious problems exist and need to be solved. *Effective control of inventory requires balancing the total of inputs to it with the total of outputs from it.*

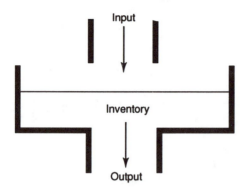

Figure 2–2 How Inventory is Really Controlled

Balancing input and output has critical timing requirements; the longer the interval in which these are out of balance, the greater will be their effects on inventory. The amounts of excess inventory (or shortages, which are "negative" inventory) will be proportional to the amount of imbalance of inputs and outputs. Few executives understand this statement:

If you cannot control the balance of input and output, you cannot control inventory.

Even more difficult to understand is the corollary:

The tighter you can control this balance, the less you need the inventory.

Excesses and shortages cannot be minimized by application of techniques to individual items, however powerful or sophisticated these may be. If the timing of input and output is faulty and the aggregate amounts of input and output cannot be matched, excesses and shortages will exist. Conversely, excesses and shortages will not occur if the timing is right and the totals balance. The closer the match between input and output in any time period, the less need there is for cushions of inventory.

The Lead Time Syndrome

The time required to procure or produce items, called cycle or lead time, is even less well managed. Executives rarely ask, or even think about, why it takes so long to make things in their companies. Managers, planners, and production workers who are conscious of the importance of lead time are sure that taking even longer would be better.

Few take time to think through the effects of adjusting lead times in the formal system. Figure 2–3 shows the sequence of the principal events; these are essentially the same for both purchased and manufactured items.

Here is a typical scenario:

1. At some time in every facility, it becomes evident that the work load exceeds available capacity. The current load of work cannot be completed in the planned time periods.
2. The obvious conclusion is that the planned lead times, whether for purchased or manufactured items, are too short. These are immediately increased.
3. When this is done, ordering systems react quickly to generate more orders which are released to plant or supplier.
4. A four-week increase in planned lead time will produce at least four weeks of additional work for suppliers and work centers. When these are released, existing backlogs grow larger.
5. With larger backlogs, actual lead times grow longer.
6. Longer lead times cause plans to be less valid, control of priorities becomes more difficult and shortages increase.

The excess of load over capacity persists, perhaps becoming even larger if extra cushions of materials are ordered by people reacting to higher levels of uncertainty over longer lead times. The situation has worsened but the overload triggers another trip around the vicious cycle shown in Figure 2–3.

Figure 2–3 The Lead Time Syndrome

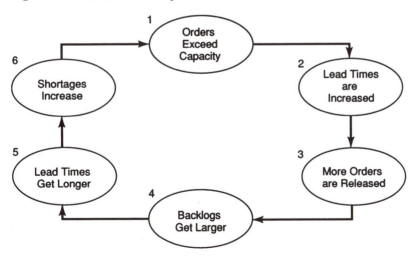

Another increase will be made in planned lead times, generating more excess orders and work-in-process and more shortages. After several such cycles, lead times will be months or even years in length, plans will become invalid, inventories of excess materials and open order backlogs will be very high at the same time that shortages of specific items will be acute. More of the wrong stuff will be made.

Viewing the increased order rates, people unaware of the true situation will be convinced that an upturn is occurring in the business cycle. It will seem obvious that more production capacity is needed and plant expansion, even whole new plants will be started.

When actual output rates equal apparent demand, the lead time increases will end. The flow of new orders will then slow down, providing clear evidence to those unfamiliar with the syndrome that the business cycle is at its peak, and a downturn will soon follow. Caution is indicated, and some orders may be rescheduled or canceled.

Reduced input will cause work loads to drop below available capacity. Suppliers will attempt to attract new business to keep capacity filled by quoting shorter lead times. Company planners will direct cuts in capacity to avoid idle time.

Customers will react to shorter lead times by deferring new or canceling existing orders. This, together with capacity cutbacks internally in many companies, will convince viewers that a recession has begun. The inevitable response of even fewer orders and greater cuts in output will soon make this a reality.

I called this the Lead Time Syndrome in two of my books (Bibl. 16, 18) which contain details of how to overcome, even prevent, it. It has occurred several times for every industrial commodity over the last two decades. It has had major effects on the economies of whole nations. It almost destroyed the semiconductor industry three times within a 15-year period. It has been a principal cause of the decline of the U.S. machine tool industry. The root problem is the lack of full understanding of how manufacturing works and how to control it.

THE SITUATION TODAY

Modern computer systems are viewed as culprits by some managers and victims by others. Both are wrong. Systems are not panaceas; neither are they negligible factors. In many companies today, formal planning and control systems are still used simply to provide paperwork authorizing what people have decided to do based on information given them by informal systems. The human animal is distinguished from all others by its ingenuity in developing and using tools to enhance its physical and mental capabilities and in adapting to its environment. Nowhere is ingenuity, innovation, and adaptability more clearly evident than in the informal systems and crises responses of people lacking formal systems capable of helping them run manufacturing.

Inadequate technical capabilities of the formal system are rarely the most urgent problem. Planning to make more than facilities can handle, inaccurate data, poor product design, bad information on customers' true needs, and suppliers' real capabilities and lack of teamwork among major functions are the culprits. Very few executives have had experience running a business with a good system, or even know how to do it.

Problems with the design of the formal system, however, have been common. Fragmented, stand-alone subsystems have been set up in engineering, marketing, and accounting departments which are not linked directly to planning and control systems. Simulation capabilities have not been made available in formal systems to test the effects of alternative decisions. Sophistication, complexity, and lack of good user documentation make it difficult for people to know when to follow the systems' recommendations closely and when to take other permissible actions.

The sophistication and complexity of business systems has resulted from attempts to build into them the ability to handle many kinds of aberrant conditions. Unpredictable scrap losses require factors to increase requirements or scheduling larger lots to offset losses. Large numbers of open work orders on the plant floor demand fast, powerful data collection capability to track progress. Frequent engineering changes initiate complex analyses to identify their effects on operations. These are all attempts to treat symptoms of serious underlying problems. They don't work, however sophisticated they are. Much better results will be obtained by attacking the base problems. This principle is appropriate:

6. Well-run operations do not require complex systems.

Claims of tremendous system capabilities have oversold replanning as desirable, implying that systems so used will help people cope better with upsets and changes. The real need for cleaning up the environment and taking steps to improve execution to get back on plan have been ignored or, at best, played down until the latter years of the 1980s.

Top-level executives who have marketing, financial, or other non-manufacturing backgrounds believe that a knowledge of "how to read the numbers" qualifies them to run any company. The measures of performance which they think appropriate are customer service, labor efficiency, machine utilization, inventory turnover, and budgeted overhead costs.

They view production operations as technical, frustratingly detailed activities which require a lot of invested capital and generate the bulk of costs. They believe that good technicians and powerful computers are the requirements for good performance and treat the technicians as second class citizens in management. Production managers are rarely invited to participate in discussions about corporate strategy, and physical capital budgets are their only contribution to long-term planning.

The lack of understanding by such top-level executives of how manufacturing can and should be run leads to some very bad decisions. When companies are poorly operated, knowing little or nothing of how to evaluate whether or not they could be developed into worldwide competitors, financially oriented managers sell off assets in an attempt to keep earnings high. Bethlehem Steel is a classic example of this. Based on this fallacy—that plant operations cannot be made competitive—divestitures of companies that could have been salvaged have cost millions of dollars that would have been better spent on their rehabilitation.

The high-tech electronics businesses, touted heavily as America's future, are proving to be no substitute for the heavy metal, smokestack-type industries of the 1960s and 1970s. They create fewer jobs, pay lower wages, and are themselves falling victim to international competition.

Meeting the major objectives of giving customers satisfaction, making adequate profits, and managing capital assets better in today's global economy is possible for practically every company in America. The ways to do these are known and tested.However, such knowledge is conspicuous today by its absence in many companies' management.

The growing importance of becoming more competitive is obvious. Competition is now global. To succeed, a U.S. manufacturing company must

* Build products in the United States competitive with other domestic producers.
* Build products in the United States competitive with foreign imports.
* Build products in other countries competitive with native makers and foreign imports.

It is not yet too late to arrest the decline of U.S. industry and make it a leading competitor again. American manufacturers can succeed or fail, depending on how soon management gets smart and busy.

CHAPTER 3

Manufacturing as a Process

The most visible waste is not scrap but good materials sitting idle.

SUMMARY

To control it properly, manufacturing must be seen as a single process involving the flow of materials from suppliers through a company to its customers and flows of information into, through and out of an integrated planning and control system linking all activities. The better it runs, the simpler the systems required. The commonly recognized objectives are customer satisfaction, adequate profits and well-managed capital assets, but others must be added related to being a good citizen of the economic and social communities of which firms are members.

Tremendous diversity, many technologies, a multitude of skills, and masses of data cause nonmanufacturing executives to be overly dependent on specialists and to compartmentalize activities, both of which cause unnecessary problems.

Manufacturing can be classified in many ways; for our purposes, the most useful is by type of process used. While many differences exist, manufacturing companies have many common characteristics, some clear to all and some not easy for the uninitiated to see. Unique systems are unnecessary and wasteful.

The five requirements for effective control are realistic planning, high data integrity, timely feedback, sound analyses, and fast correction. Flows of material and information are often interrupted by many problems; all can be attacked successfully. Continuous efforts must be exerted to smooth out, speed up, and improve the quality of both flows. The definition of waste now includes many factors in addition to scrap. The causes must be found and fixed. This requires everyone's efforts, teamwork among groups and strong leadership by management. Manufacturing is truly a process, complex in details but simple in essence.

MANUFACTURING IS A PROCESS

To control it properly and to gain maximum flexibility in reacting to changes, manufacturing must be viewed as a single process encompassing a company's suppliers, all of its internal activities, and its customers. All planning and control, internal and external, must be integrated in a single system illustrated in Figure 1–1 and discussed in Chapters 1 and 5.

As was noted in Chapter 1, this does not require a unique, supersophisticated, massive computer system; the better the operations are run, the simpler the system required. A core system and many subsystems, cataloged in Chapter 5, will make up the whole. Such subsystems are logical parts of the formal system and make it easier to understand, develop, install, and operate the total system. They must be tightly integrated to function smoothly together, just as the separate parts of a human body need a single brain to coordinate all functions. Compartmentalizing parts of the process in isolated, independent subsystems will result in much poorer performance, possibly failure.

OBJECTIVES OF MANUFACTURING

Asked what the primary objectives of manufacturing companies are, most people in and out of industry would reply, "Make the maximum profits, dominate its markets, and pay maximum dividends." The primary objectives all manufacturing companies should have were identified by Henry Ford in 1926 in his classic book, *Today and Tomorrow*, (Bibl. 6). Figure 3–1 lists these in Ford's order of importance based on his emphasis and the amount of coverage in the book. These are once again recognized as the important goals for companies desiring to be world-class leaders in their industries.

Satisfy Customers Completely

Good customer service has long been a primary objective of many manufacturers. The definition has changed significantly, however, along with the word "service" which is now "satisfaction" or even

Satisfy Customers Completely

Earn Adequate Profits

Use Capital Effectively

Generate More Wealth

Reward Participants Equitably

Treat Suppliers and Customers Fairly

Be a Good Citizen

Figure 3-1 Manufacturing Objectives

"delight." From meeting specifications and delivery dates reasonably well, the criteria now include anything relevant to ensuring complete customer satisfaction. Customer satisfaction can be evaluated by various measures, some are simple percentages of on-time delivery, some are complex calculations of many factors. The best measure is the customers' evaluation.

Achieving full customer satisfaction imposes several important objectives on producers' relationships with customers:

* Produce the highest quality products possible.
* Produce what they really need when they need it.
* Deliver it to their desired location.
* Produce the lowest cost products suitable.
* React flexibly and fast to changes in needs.

Practically every manufacturing business is a customer as well as a supplier of materials. Relations with customers, however, are almost invariably viewed very differently from those with suppliers. This is just one more fallacy. There is no real difference between the two situations; whether buying or selling, the partners' relationships are the same. Very significant mutual benefits are available if this is seen clearly.

Arm's-length and adversarial relationships, typical of most customer/company relations in the past, prevented complete and open communications between the two. Customers desiring goods and services told suppliers specifically what they wanted and when it was needed via individual purchase orders placed far in advance; these were often almost pure fiction.

Uncertainty about supplier's quality and poor delivery causes customers to pad orders, asking for more materials to be delivered sooner than really needed. Their failure to expedite many late orders provides clear evidence to suppliers that such padding exists. Suppliers, in turn, work to schedules suiting their own best interests rather than customers' needs. Poor communication results in poor performance—material shortages and excess, unusable inventories occurring simultaneously—both expensive and both damaging to supplier and customer.

Earn Adequate Profits

To be successful, a firm's products and services must represent value to customers higher than the manufacturers' costs; the difference is the suppliers' profits. Higher profit is often viewed by many executives as the most important objective of manufacturing companies. It should not be. Profit is important, of course, even necessary for survival in free-enterprise economies. Instead of being the primary objective, however, it should be viewed simply as one measure of how well a company is being operated. Well-run companies will make adequate profits; those whose primary goal is profit often have trouble surviving.

Letting specific profit goals dominate actions detracts from achieving other objectives more important to the future health and life of the firm. The focus on short-term results has handicapped U. S. companies attempting to compete with European and Pacific Rim producers who think more deeply about the long-term effects of today's actions.

Use Capital Effectively

Asset management is the objective meeting with the least success of the primary goals. The more attention it gets from executives, the worse their performance. Every company has an inventory budget; few meet it consistently. Even worse, it is a rare inventory budget that bears any relation to detailed plans of operation; most are based on improving turnover or recapturing invested capital now needed elsewhere, as if inventory were an independent variable. It is always called an asset but invariably treated as a liability. The great bulk of inventory in manufacturing companies, at least 75% by a very conservative estimate, is not being worked on or in use; it is sitting idly in storerooms, plants, and warehouses tying up capital needed elsewhere and adding unnecessary costs.

The utilization of other capital assets, machinery, tooling, test or inspection equipment, and other production hardware, is better; in fact, in some firms it may be too high. Conventional executive wisdom maintains that "expensive machinery should never be idle." This fails to recognize the resultant extreme penalties of even small temporary overloads—poor customer service, excess inventory, and high costs. It also ignores the value of available open capacity to increase flexibility to react quickly to changes and to capture more new business. The dictum may also incur immediate excess costs when the wrong parts are processed on expensive machinery, or made too soon, just to keep it busy.

The profit and capital objectives are usually combined in a ratio called "Return on ...." with several different values of the capital used— assets, stockholders' equity, capital employed, and investment. Chapter 7 contains more detailed and complete coverage of these and other performance measures.

Present accounting conventions treat as expenses many items (maintenance spare parts and computer-based planning and control systems, for example) which are just as qualified by function to be capital investments as are plant and machinery and more so than accounts receivable. Current unsound accounting approaches handicap good asset management; poor decisions are the result. Chapter 7 has more on this subject.

Generate More Wealth

By adding value to lower cost materials, manufacturers generate real wealth for the societies and countries in which they operate. Simply adding value to materials, however, is not wealth generation. Products must be saleable; they must provide value at least equal to their costs to customers. The importance of this role of industry in wealth generation seems to be lost on politicians, financiers, educators, and environmentalists and is conspicuous by its absence from mention in the media. The contrast with its recognition in the Pacific Rim countries is striking. Advocates of a better balance are urgently needed; they must come from the ranks of executives, managers, and other vocal people in industry.

Reward Participants Equitably

Those who contribute to the success of manufacturing companies include workers, management, and the owners; all must receive a share of the gains. The real problem is determining the proper share for each; this is beyond the scope of this book. The failure of socialism in Europe and South America, the destruction of Eastern Airlines, and the back-breaking load of debt carried by many firms after indulging in financial games all show clearly the price paid for failure to reward all participants equitably.

Treat Suppliers and Customers Fairly

As Figure 1–1 in Chapter 1 showed, the chain of material flow in manufacturing includes suppliers, the manufacturer and customers. As Benjamin Franklin mentioned about himself and his peers at the time of the American Revolution, "We must all hang together or, surely, we shall all hang separately." The interests of all three links in the chain of manufacturing materials are common. The needs of each are served better when all prosper. Adversarial, cutthroat relations are giving way to long-term partnerships. The effects of these are treated in Chapter 6.

Be a Good Citizen

States, cities, and towns lacking a sound industrial tax base extend special offers to attract manufacturing companies. Little is said in such offers about pollution, health hazards, or excessive development as a threat to the environment, in spite of industry's poor reputation on these factors.

The important economic benefits cannot be allowed to overshadow the duties of manufacturers as good citizens. These duties must include generating real wealth, bearing a fair share of the financial burdens of society through taxes and charitable contributions, and making continuous efforts to reduce air and water pollution, degradation of the environment, and health hazards to both workers and other citizens.

The last three noneconomic objectives recognize the broader role manufacturing must play in society. They are subordinate to the four economic objectives only in the sense that good economic performance is a prerequisite to achieving good citizenship.

DIFFERENCES ARE EVIDENT

It is impossible to exaggerate the tremendous diversity of manufacturing activities. Products, materials, process machinery and equipment, sources, markets, and distribution channels are all present in unbelievable variety. A layperson not familiar with even simple products like the wooden pencil shown in Figure 3–2 will always underestimate the number of different components to be procured and processes to be controlled to make them.

Many highly complex technologies and skills are used, requiring the services of specialists. Masses of data need to be handled and processed rapidly, dictating the need for fast, high-powered computing, transmission, and printing equipment. The techniques of modern forecasting, inventory management, and production control employ sophisticated statistical and highly mathematical calculations understood thoroughly only by the professionals in those fields. Similarities are buried in a welter of differences. It is little wonder that executives who direct manufacturing businesses turn responsibility for detailed operations over to specialists.

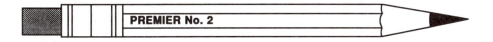

Components

Eraser - 3 Hardnesses

Ferrule - 5 Colors

Wood Barrel - Round, Hexagonal

Graphite - 5 Hardnesses

Glue - 2 Types

Paint - 5 Colors

Ink - 2 Colors

Box - 3 Sizes

Labels - 120 Brands

Cartons - 3 Sizes

Processes

Eraser - Cut to Length

Ferrule - Blank, Roll, Stake

Wood Barrel - Saw, Mill

Graphite - Cut to Length

Pencil - Assemble, Paint, Print, Sharpen

Package - Box, Label, Carton

Figure 3-2 Complexity of Pencils

One chief executive officer expressed to me the opinions of many top-level peers when he said, "I understand why marketing cannot predict accurately what customers will order, nor can they foresee the changes which will occur in our dynamic marketplace. I understand also the difficulties engineering faces in designing our state-of-the-art products and why frequent design changes are necessary, even occasional recalls of products for rework. Problems in these areas are inevitable. In spite of these, I expect production to react fast, to get deliveries out on time, to hold costs down, and to keep inventory low. That's their job. That's what we hired these high-priced experts to do."

Obviously, the three functions of marketing, engineering, and production were separate and distinct in his mind and worked independently. The first two faced problems they could not be expected to solve but the third, if qualified, should cope adequately with theirs. He saw no need for close coordination of all three since he didn't recognize that many of the problems in each were caused by the others. This compartmentalized view of manufacturing is widespread and shows a complete lack of understanding of how the manufacturing process really works.

USEFUL CLASSIFICATIONS

All manufacturing involves materials taken from the air, sea, or earth originally, altered by some processes using people and production equipment and transported to other locations for further processing or use. There are various ways in which manufacturing businesses are classified including size; types of products, processes, and materials; degree of government control; and many others. Standard Industry Code (SIC) numbers are used by the Department of Commerce of the United States to catalog useful statistics on businesses based on many different characteristics. Unfortunately, these perpetuate ideas on how different manufacturing operations are and inhibit cross-fertilization of planning and control knowledge.

To aid in understanding manufacturing as an integrated process, the most useful classes are by type of production. The significant types are

* Custom-built or job shop (few of a kind)
* Batch or intermittent (many varieties, low volume)
* Process or continuous (few varieties, high volume)
* Repetitive (few varieties, high volume)
* Controlled—tightly regulated by government (food, atomic energy, pharmaceutical, aerospace, defense, health products, utilities)

COMMON CHARACTERISTICS

Most people who write and talk about companies in various industries, and most who manage and work in them, believe that their company and their industry are significantly different from others and that these differences require fundamentally different planning and control activities. This is not true. Each company is unique, of course, just as each person is different from all others in some way. However, all people have virtually the same skeleton, vital organs, limbs, and torso, suffer from the same diseases, and can benefit from the same medicine and therapy.

In manufacturing firms, basic objectives, measures of performance, relations to customers and suppliers, internal activities and the systems by which these are planned and controlled are remarkably similar *when they are well understood*. Failing to recognize these common characteristics in humans or manufacturing companies will subject them both to very serious handicaps in their efforts to survive and prosper. We must focus first on the similarities.

The basic objectives of manufacturing identified earlier in this chapter are certainly common to all, even if the importance of each may differ from company to company and from time to time. All have customers and suppliers. Each uses people with special skills and abilities and machines and equipment in factories. All are engaged in the process of converting lower-cost materials to higher-value products.

The most important common characteristic of manufacturing companies is recognized in the following principle:

7. Manufacturing is a process involving two flows: materials and information.

These two basic flows are common to all types of manufacturing businesses. Materials flow from suppliers through a company's production operations and inventories to customers. Information relating to planning, control, and execution activities flows through closed-loop systems linking suppliers, companies, and customers and can be relayed to owners, managers, government, and the public. The two flows are represented graphically in Figure 1–1 in Chapter 1.

In spite of the great multitude of differences among businesses, focusing on these two common streams permits the formulation of a useful law of planning and control which can be applied to all types. The common factors far outweigh the unique features of individual firms and provide the bases for improving planning and control and achieving better performance.

Prominent among the common features of all manufacturing companies are the many files of data needed. These include

* Bills of material—detailing the components of products and showing parent/component relations
* Costs, actual and budgeted—showing the price of materials, people's wages and salaries, energy, and other fixed and variable costs
* Customers' orders, actual and forecasted—specifying models, quantities, delivery dates, and other relevant factors
* Material inventories available—showing quantities active, excess, and obsolete for each item
* Manufacturing orders, released and planned—to make additional quantities of active items
* Purchase orders, released and planned—to procure additional quantities of active items
* Subcontract orders—to get the services of outside firms in producing goods and services
* Physical assets, available and planned—plant, machinery, equipment, tooling, and other property
* Processing methods—describing how manufactured items are made and where the work is done
* Quality data—identifying acceptable and rejected materials and services

These data are the raw materials used by planning and control systems in all manufacturing firms. It seems at best wasteful and at worst useless to develop unique subsystems to maintain such data files differently in different companies.

INFORMATION FLOW REQUIREMENTS

Effective control of manufacturing, covered in more detail in Chapter 6, has five requirements:

* Realistic planning—capable of being executed
* Data integrity—everyone can believe the numbers
* Timely feedback—prompt comparisons of performance against plan
* Sound analyses—competent people distinguishing clearly between basic problems and symptoms
* Fast correction—permanent corrections made quickly

These use the two sets of numbers representing planned and actual performance. Planned data are realistic when two criteria are met: the planning horizon is very short and resources are or will be available to execute the plan. Plans lose validity rapidly as projections are made farther into the future. Computer-based systems are capable of handling planning over long horizons; the real question is whether or not it is necessary or worthwhile to do so. This is covered more fully in Chapter 6.

The quality of data used in many manufacturing operations varies from poor to terrible. Often 50% of the data found in the files have significant errors, and no one knows which 50% it is! As explained in Chapter 7, this can be corrected quickly, inexpensively, and permanently. Eliminating errors can add significant tangible benefits to the bottom line of the profit and loss statement quickly; even if this were not true, *errors must be eliminated if planning and control systems are to be viable.*

Modern data collection and processing equipment are capable of providing instantaneous reporting of performance and variance from plan on thousands of activities. There are no longer any valid excuses for essential control information being delayed and becoming ancient history. Timely signals of problems are vital; *promptness is more important than completeness.* The availability of this data-handling power, however, has tempted too many people to track trivia. Often, more data are not better than fewer.

In manufacturing problems as in human diseases, it is easy to detect symptoms; it requires a trained individual to diagnose the real source of the difficulty. Failure to spot the true source of the trouble and tinkering with symptoms frequently aggravates the situation and adds more problems.

This is the cause of the failure of daily crisis (so-called "production" or "7:30 A.M.") meetings to improve operations; expediting and firefighting generate at least as many problems as they solve. Even more important, permanent solutions of chronic problems can never be achieved without attacking and eliminating the basic causes; this requires a skilled, experienced team of people.

People charged with determining the few underlying causes of the multitude of symptoms need a smooth, fast flow of very-high-quality information. Computer-based systems must be instructed to distinguish important information from masses of data, producing exception reports showing significant deviations and suppressing trivial ones. Chapter 7 has more details on how this can be done effectively.

MATERIAL FLOW REQUIREMENTS

Many problems cause interruptions in material flow and interfere with achieving desired performance goals. The consensus of most manufacturing people has long been that such problems were indigenous to the environment. President Harry Truman's famous comment about the problems of the presidency, "If you don't like the heat, get out of the kitchen," has been deemed apt. Contrary to this attitude, the accepted principle now is

8. No manufacturing problem is unsolvable.

It is impossible to limit the effects of serious chronic problems remaining unsolved. Delays in finding and fixing problems blocking flow result in more aggravated constipation affecting more products, more costs, more capital investment, and more customers. Attempts to provide cushions of inventory, time, or capacity as protection against such problems are ineffective for reasons explained in Chapter 2.

In the process industry handling continuous flows of liquids and gases, problems interfering with the smooth flows of products are clearly intolerable. It is oversimplified (but not greatly) to say that all manufacturing plants must strive to approach process plants in achieving constant flow of materials. Faster and smoother flows of materials are vital to good performance in every manufacturing company; *the flow can be smoothed out and speeded up in any company.*

The sequence of required actions to accomplish this is

* Get broad acceptance of the concept throughout the whole organization—materials sitting idle are anathema.
* Recognize operation sequences where balanced rates can be achieved and arrange machines in flow lines or cells.
* Develop more level production schedules—use daily rates for families of similar items in lieu of individual orders for batches of specific parts.

   * Attack setup and changeover times for major reductions—95% cuts are possible quickly with little capital investment in tooling or machinery.

   * Reduce production lot quantities—the ideal is the amount needed each day for customers' orders.

   * Feed a constant amount of work to plant work centers and to suppliers.

   * Insist on plant and suppliers meeting daily rates and recovering quickly from falldowns.

   * Build flexibility into all activities to permit quick reaction to the inevitable changes.

   * Enlist everyone in the early detection and swift solution of problems affecting smooth, fast flow.

   * Keep at it doggedly, patiently, and endlessly.

The technical aspects of these actions are easy, simple and not expensive. These are covered in more detail in my articles (Bibl. 17, 20) and books (Bibl. 16, 18, 19). The real difficulties are encountered in changing the mind-set of people to accept the need for doing them and the possibility that they will work in their company.

ATTACKS ON WASTE

A result of the overall view of manufacturing as a process is the broadening definition of waste. Conventional wisdom of the past focused on three principal wastes: material scrapped, idle workers' time, and low machine utilization. Chapter 7 covers some real harm that results from rigorous use of these measures of performance. Accepted practices of the past are now seen as generators of waste.

The Toyota production system described in Shigeo Shingo's book (Bibl. 25) identified seven causes of waste:

1. Overproduction—components and products made in excess of immediate needs. Controlling this waste requires developing level schedules (process steps can be balanced better) and short setup times (small batches are economical).

2. Delays—material or information stalled, not flowing. There are many causes, all deemed avoidable.

3. Transportation—movement of materials over distances. This involves plant layout, subcontract work, and procurement from distant suppliers.

4. Processing—unnecessary operations. Product design, process technology, robotics, and automation help.

5. Excess inventory—materials beyond immediate needs and cushions for protection against upsets are anathema.

6. Motions—unnecessary human activity. The ultimate goal is elimination of human effort.

7. Defects—substandard materials and information. The goal is perfection at the source.

For a complete list, I would add three more:

8. Time—procrastination in decision making and taking action. Keeping ahead of competitors in a more rapidly changing environment requires fast responses.

9. People—unused skills and abilities. This aims at getting full use of this unique resource.

10. Paperwork—redundant and unneeded reports. These are symptoms of serious problems in organization, measures of performance and control points.

Reducing these wastes will require the efforts of every person in the organization, close cooperation between departments and functions, and strong leadership and direction by executives.

Manufacturing is truly a process. When viewed properly, the importance of smoothing out and speeding up the flow of both materials and information becomes obvious. Combined with attacks on problems which interfere with producing very-high-quality goods, cause interruptions in production, and increase costs, planning and control are simplified and become more effective. In addition, flexibility to meet inevitable changes is enhanced. The paradox is that manufacturing is extremely complex in its details but essentially simple in essence.

CHAPTER 4

Strategic Planning

The battle is lost before it begins if the army, navy, and air force strategies differ.

SUMMARY

Long-range planning is a common management activity requiring considerable time and effort but producing little of use in daily operations. Individual departments prefer to operate independently, rarely following a common strategy. A hierarchy of four major groups of plans is necessary to ensure teamwork among these functions.

Strategic planning states the charter of the business, identifies major markets, lays out long-term goals and objectives, and develops coordinated strategies for all functions. Strategic plans are not definitive but establish ranges and include contingency plans to be followed if the unexpected occurs. Business planning focuses on product families and actions to be taken to improve share of market. Production planning covers the physical and financial resources needed to support the strategic and business plans. The master production schedule specifies details of future production and drives detailed operating plans, the bases for coordination and control of all activities.

The definition of the business charter has a great effect on all planning. To develop teamwork, strategies for the individual functions must be compatible. Production can be made a powerful weapon in competitive battles if sound strategies are followed. Subordinate to the common strategies, each department can have a number of other strategies to follow.

Master scheduling, the process of developing the master production schedule, must become an important executive activity. Regular, rigorous reviews of these important numbers can ensure tight control of operations. The hierarchy of plans provides executives with "control handles" by which they can move the business in desired directions.

THE PLANNING HIERARCHY

Industrial companies need a variety of types of plans. Most management groups spend significant amounts of time preparing these plans, particularly as part of the annual budgeting process. Much thought is given to the aptness of the charter of the business, to increases in market share, to the development of new and improved products, and to investments in more and better facilities to produce them. The introduction of new technologies in both products and processes is studied. Policies are established for customer service, stable employment, and other goals.

Each business function—engineering, marketing, production, and finance—considers matters carefully in its own areas of responsibility and expertise and these different considerations are merged into an integrated plan expressed in financial terms. The result, typically called "the long-range plan," is produced in a voluminous report and distributed to all managers who have a need to know and act on it. Unfortunately, most copies are then carefully filed, not to be viewed again until just prior to next year's planning meeting. The functional groups go about their daily activities, and any resemblance between these and the long-range plan are mainly coincidental.

Most companies lack true integration of long-range plans with those for detailed operations. When this is so, individual functions subordinate long-range plan goals and policies to the exigencies of day-to-day pressures and crises. This is not too strong an indictment of the planning process in many firms.

In the long-range planning process, basic agreement is developed, after heated discussion of some topics, on such objectives as profits, rate of growth, customer service, share of market, and return on investment. Serious differences arise among managers of the different functions, however, and are rarely resolved, in *determining the specific actions each should take* to reach these commonly agreed objectives. Marketing people believe that an increase in market share and profits depends upon offering a wider variety of lower cost products, introducing new models more frequently and quickly, having all necessary spare parts and adequate amounts of finished goods always in stock, and making on-time deliveries to customers.

People in research and development and design engineering prefer to operate at their own deliberate paces to develop state-of-the-art products with only minimal attention to marketability, timing and pro-ducibility. To meet profit and return-on-investment goals in which they play the major role, production people press for more accurate forecasts, more stable plans, higher selling prices, fewer product models and engi-neering changes, and longer time between new product introductions.

It is obvious that these groups are not operating to common strategies but, in fact, are diverging. This is more typical of activities in most companies than is commonly believed. If companies are to perform at their best, the major functions cannot be allowed to operate independently with the inevitable conflict of interests interfering with the effective execution of all plans. Excellence in operations requires an integrated, orderly hierarchy of master plans supported by detailed functional plans. Four basic levels of plans are needed, each covered in detail later in this chapter:

* Strategic plans
* Business plans
* Production plans
* Master production schedules

Strategic planning starts with a definition of the nature of the business, usually called its "charter." **Strategic plans** identify the major markets the company desires to serve and also specify the strategies to be followed by the functions of the business. An important objective, too often overlooked, is to ensure that these strategies are compatible. Stra-tegic plans usually cover a horizon of five years; the accelerating rate of change in markets and technologies often makes this too far out.

Business plans cover a much shorter horizon, less than five years, often only two. They concentrate on product families, individual product life cycles, and company market share. They must be consistent with product data in the front end of strategic plans. They and the **production plans** are numerical statements of how the strategies will be carried out. The former focuses on products to be offered and the latter on the facilities to produce them. Each is made in five phases, covering the individual activities of research and development, design engineering, marketing, production, and finance.

R&D business and production plans focus on applying new technol-ogies to both products and processes. In production and finance they may be combined into one plan for each function. Design engineering develops new products and major improvements in existing ones as well as assist-ing production in the application of new process technologies. Marketing plans define marketplaces, methods of achieving targeted share of mar-ket, channels of distribution, desired customer service levels, anticipated sales of products, future market needs, and rates of growth anticipated.

Production plans identify present and needed resources of plant and equipment, materials, and people to support the market needs. Financial plans indicate how needed capital will be obtained and what controls will be used to monitor how well the business is being managed.

The first year's data in these plans provide information to those concerned with hiring and developing people, procuring materials, buying short-lead-time equipment, making the products, planning inventory levels, and detailed budgeting. Data for the second and subsequent years are used by those responsible for getting critical raw materials, long-delivery equipment, and additional plant space; developing new markets and products; expanding the distribution network; and introducing new technologies. The need for careful integration of these business and production plans cannot be overemphasized.

The **master production schedule** states specifically which products will be manufactured, how many will be produced, and when they will be built. This is one of the most important sets of numbers used in operating a manufacturing business. The detailed plans developed from this set of numbers provides the sheet music by which all people can perform in concert.

All of these plans in the hierarchy must be coordinated timewise as shown in Figure 4–1. Production plans rarely extend more than two years into the future and it is now rare to find master production schedules more than one year out; most are six months and many are even shorter.

Management time spent in preparing these plans and monitoring progress against them will have major impacts on the health and success

Figure 4–1 Planning Time Relationships

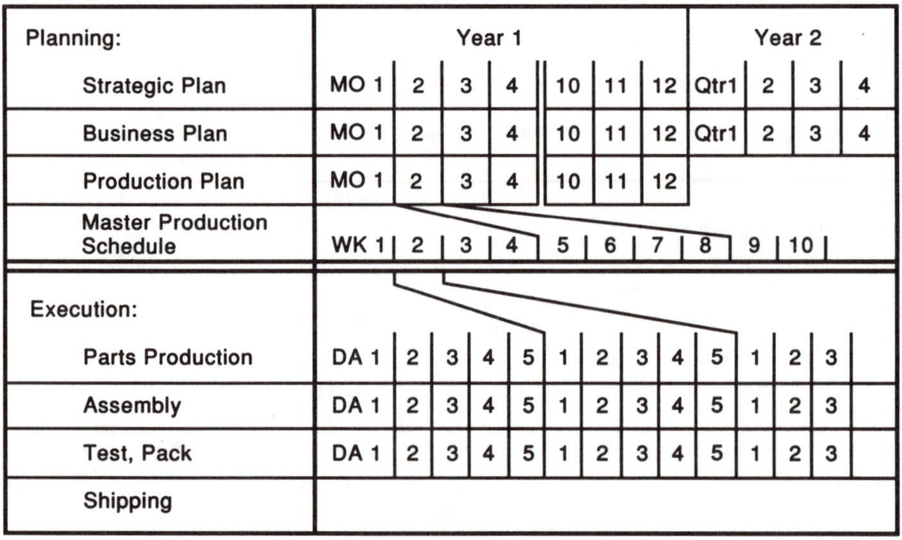

of the business. This process, which I call "master planning," is often done only partially. Executives spend time planning but usually neglect to compare performance to plans regularly.

Nonmanufacturing executives spend far too little time comparing actual business' performance to production plans and master production schedules and ensuring that these vital plans are valid. A specific section at the end of this chapter discusses this role of top management.

STRATEGIC PLANNING

One of Confucius' familiar statements is that a journey of 1,000 miles begins with a single step. The direction of that and all subsequent steps is as important as the decision to take the first one. Strategic planning is the process of deciding on this direction and ensuring that the people in the organization know where they are heading and use their skills and abilities to get there together.

Strategic plans attempt to answer the following questions:

* What business are we in now?
* What markets do we serve now?
* What business do we want to be in? By when?
* What other markets should we serve?
* What must be done now to get ready? In research and development? In engineering? In marketing? In finance? In production?
* What will be required next from these functions?
* Do these functions have compatible strategies?

Many managers accept the futility of attempting to make projections for their businesses more than a year in the future and do only a cursory, superficial job of attempting to identify future events which can affect their businesses significantly. Sound strategic planning does not attempt to identify a single set of data describing the situation five or more years hence.

Attempts to predict specifically what will happen a year or more in the future are futile exercises in magic numbers. The best that can be done is to *make reasonable estimates of the ranges over which significant factors may vary and the future effects of current decisions.* From these estimates, possible alternative courses of future actions can be identified now, and contingency plans can be made in advance. This is far better than last-minute reactions to unexpected crises.

The best starting point in strategic planning is developing a clear statement of the charter of the business, defining the type of business the company conducts. Too often management identifies this with the products now being made rather than the services provided—"we are in the forklift truck business" instead of "we provide equipment to move industrial materials" or "we make electronic home appliances" instead of "we make products to help people in their homes." Taking too narrow a view risks failure to take advantage of new product and new market opportunities. It is interesting to speculate about how U.S. railroads would have developed had they seen their business not as simply "running a railroad" but as "providing low-cost, long-distance transportation of people and materials." In the charter statement, the customers to be served, their desires, and their preferences must be the primary consideration.

When manufacturers sell through distributors to the final users of their products, they must consider the desires of both. FireKing International Company met both types of customers' needs with its fireproof filing cabinets. They set up their own contract freight carriers to minimize freight costs, offered a prepaid freight program, enhanced their Underwriters Laboratories ratings, provided more scratch-resistant finishes, and designed more attractive casings. Their strategy was, "Have the best products for the users; be the most profitable supplier for the dealers." The result was a 24% compound annual growth rate over 13 years and a move from last to first place against five competitors.

Sound strategic planning requires careful coordination of the work of the various functions. Research and development efforts must, of course, precede application design. Coordination of marketing and design engineering ensures that products will have strong market impact and serve the real needs of customers. Engineering designs must be completed *and proved sound* in time for procurement of necessary tooling, materials, and other manufacturing resources, and production and sales teamwork will have products ready when customers' orders require them.

The rapid pace of changes in customers' expectations, in expanding global markets, in the introduction of new materials and development of new processing methods have shortened product life cycles from a range of 5 to 15 years in the 1950s to only 1 to 3 years in the 1980s. This will continue in the twenty-first century. High-volume output of a few varieties of products, economies of scale, and long development and learning curves are gone forever. A steady flow of new and better products brought quickly to market must be paramount in strategic planning. Too little capital invested in research and development will be as fatal as poor-quality products or failure to control costs.

For too long, management has been tolerant of the inability of research and development and design engineering people to work fast and to adhere to schedules. The U.S. space program, many military projects, and breakthrough computer developments have all proven that tight schedules can be adhered to even for products not yet invented. The need for speed cannot be used as a reason to avoid responsibility for a sound design, however. General Electric found out how high the cost can be when a new compressor unit for refrigerators was released for production before adequate testing. The benefits of fast development were lost several times over in the recall/repair costs. *Speedy and sound design is the goal.*

Time is the one resource available equally to everyone but impossible to recapture or store. Lost time is the greatest waste. Around-the-clock operations for design engineering, involving relatively few people, are far less costly and much more effective in getting and staying on schedule than overcoming delays when many individuals and activities are involved in procurement and production.

Probably the single most important objective of strategic planning is the development of a clear statement of strategy for each of the major functions and ensuring that these strategies are compatible. Engineering, marketing, sales, production, and finance must have clear directions on the strategies they are to follow; conflicts among these strategies are counterproductive. In this group, finance is particularly important because of the high interest in mergers, acquisitions, and other financial manipulations of whole corporations so prevalent in the 1980s.

Marketing strategies are usually considered quite carefully by top managers in deciding how to respond to competition and opportunities in the marketplace. They commonly see the need for more varieties of products, for new products to be developed more quickly, for short- and on-time deliveries to serve a particular market or niche in the marketplace, and for fast response to changes in both product designs and customer requirements.

It is equally common to find production people operating without any defined strategy. Executives in a client company making consumer products, in response to my question, said that they had 17 pages of their long-range plan devoted to marketing strategies (principally the ones listed in Figure 4–1) but had not even thought of a production strategy. They admitted that they measured production on its ability to keep costs under control, to develop high utilization of expensive equipment, and to meet tight budgets for direct and indirect labor. They had not realized that these defined de facto strategies (listed also in Figure 4–2); production people performing to such measures must strive to stabilize operations, will press

Figure 4–2 Comparison of Marketing and Production Strategies

1. Fast Response- Cycles, Orders	1. Stable Operations- Good Forecasts
2. More Varieties, Faster	2. Fewer Models, Longer Development
3. Short, On-Time Deliveries	3. Longer, Balanced Loads
4. Low Costs	4. High Prices

for good forecasts and long runs of a few products, and will resist the development of new products and frequent engineering changes. It is clear why their marketing people viewed the plants as "millstones around our necks"; they were operating with opposing strategies.

Add to this the desire of marketing for low costs to provide ample margins to help compete in the marketplace and production's interest in high selling prices to take the pressure off factory costs. It takes only a moment's consideration to see that the two strategies in this example, marketing's explicit and production's implicit, are directly in conflict. Competition instead of cooperation between marketing and production is very destructive of any company's efforts to be competitive.

Wickham Skinner addressed the failure of top managers to understand the true relation between marketing and production and the latter's potential as a competitive weapon in his 1969 article, "Manufacturing—Missing Link in Corporate Strategy" (Bibl. 26). It is tragic that so few nonmanufacturing managers at that time understood his message and applied it to their operations; most still do not. When executives, particularly marketing managers, tell me that their plants are millstones around their necks, I know that strategies of marketing and manufacturing are conflicting. Marketing wants to run like hares but production behaves like tortoises.

From many years of counseling, some common patterns of strategies emerge for each function. Typical of these are

Useful Strategies for Design Engineering

* Develop state-of-the-art technologies in both products and processes, as illustrated by military and defense production and so-called "high-tech" electronics.
* Ensure top performance of product functions as is so characteristic of low-volume, high-cost, high-quality automobiles and commercial aircraft.
* Introduce countercyclical products intended to offset seasonal and other cyclical products and provide more balanced use of manufacturing facilities.
* Aim for high utilization of facilities by developing new products to replace others that have become obsolete, to increase utilization of existing equipment or to utilize new facilities employing new technology.

The bulk of material and production costs, most of the inventory investment and many production problems are determined by the product design. In-depth considerations of both the functioning and manufacturability of products is essential in the design phase; too much time and effort are wasted redesigning.

Common Marketing Strategies

* Expand into regions and countries which can be supplied economically and will increase market share.
* Offer low-priced, high-volume products like household appliances and many consumer products.
* Offer limited-volume products of top-quality and high prices characteristic of luxury automobiles, watches, jewelry, and porcelain art objects.
* Produce a broad line of products in many varieties with quick and reliable delivery. This is the strategy adopted by Stanley Tools and other broad-line manufacturers striving to meet all customers' needs for their types of products so customers have no need to go to their competitors for anything.
* Produce a narrow line of few varieties with fast response to customer changes. This strategy is adopted by companies attempting to secure a niche in markets dominated by major competitors such as IBM and General Electric. Head-to-head competition with such giants is avoided and only a portion of the market is served.

Inherent in the development of marketing strategies is the knowledge of the true needs of customers. These are frequently quite different from the needs perceived by engineering and marketing people and even from the wants expressed in their orders by customers. Close and open relations with customers is essential to define their real needs correctly.

Strategies Applicable to Production

* Produce high-volume, low-cost products in limited models and varieties. This is most often seen in consumer products in so-called mass production.
* Make many models and varieties of low volume products with slow but flexible response to market changes. This is typical of heavy machinery, off-road equipment, and machine tools.
* Make high-performance items of top quality in low volumes. This is characteristic of such products as top-of-the-line automobiles, cameras, watches, and stereo sound equipment.
* Design and build custom equipment. This is the "job shop" environment making products to individual customer specifications and usually in quantities of one or two.

Attempting to perform in one factory to two or more strategies is difficult at best and can be self-defeating. Companies previously concentrating on defense and military products have had little success diversifying into consumer goods. This requires setting up separate and distinct facilities even though they may be under the same plant roof. As Wickham Skinner observed (Bibl. 26), plants making a limited line of products (focus factories) operating according to a single strategy will always perform better than will large industrial complexes.

Strategies in Finance

* Increase value per share of stock. This can require careful study of leasing versus owning capital equipment, using funds generated internally rather than entering equity markets, buying back its own stock, and selling off fixed assets.
* Increase return on capital employed. Tight budgeting of expenses, programs to reduce inventories and accounts receivable and similar actions support this strategy.
* Improve debt/equity ratio. This focuses on reducing debt by using funds generated internally.

The era of financial manipulations of manufacturing companies has not yet ended, unfortunately. Based on a fallacy—that plant operations cannot be made competitive—poorly performing companies (that could have been salvaged) have been sold and good performers purchased at inflated prices. The millions of dollars involved would have been better spent on rehabilitation. Enormous legal and banking fees in acquisitions and mergers for dubious purposes have siphoned off many more millions of dollars. At the same time, capital badly needed for improvement of manufacturing operations has been scarce and expensive. This has been a significant factor in the loss of competitive position by American corporations.

Some combinations of strategies among finance, marketing, manufacturing, and engineering are obviously very compatible and others highly competitive. Different but compatible strategies can coexist; one can apply to one line of products or market and another to an entirely different product or market.

Strategic planning should be an annual effort occupying the attention of the top level management group. It also needs to be reviewed for possible changes quarterly or no less than twice a year. The output of this planning effort should be

* A specific statement of strategy for each function for the various major families of products and markets.
* Answers to each of the questions listed for strategic planning. These answers may be specific or just a generalized statement depending on the nature of the question.
* Identification of alternative courses of action and some generalized contingency plans to handle each.
* Specific timetables for the major activities in the first year or two (depending on the type of business) of the planning horizon to be coordinated closely with the business and production planning activities to be described next.

* Identification of the performance measures to be used to determine when strategies are failing and who is responsible for corrective actions. Strategic planning without effective execution is as futile as a winning game plan in sports without the ability of team players to carry it out.

BUSINESS PLANNING

The business plan concentrates on product families and their life cycles and on market share. It must be consistent with the front end of the strategic plan. The business plan attempts to answer the following questions:

* How do our products and markets rank now?
* Which are declining? How fast?
* Which should be dropped? Now? Later?
* Which are mature, stable?
* Which are growing? How fast?
* What new products are needed? When?
* What are competitors doing? Products? Technologies? Applications?
* What actions are needed by us? When?

As with strategic planning, business planning is not intended to develop specific numbers in a time frame. Its purposes are to indicate trends, set minimum and maximum dates for introduction or ending of the production of specific products, and develop timetables and details of marketing and sales activities to improve the company's competitive position.

While it is a separate phase of planning, the business plan cannot be developed independently of the strategic plans already made; they must be tied closely together and support each other. As in strategic plans, the first one or two years at the front end of the business plan contain more detail and more specific data so that the subsequent detailed planning processes can be integrated better with them.

A specific question of business planning is the actions of competitors in introducing new products, discontinuing old ones, and developing new technologies or new applications in the marketplace. Here more specific answers are needed. The actual performance and, even more important, intentions of competitors are vital questions in determining a company's plans for its own products and markets.

Such intelligence can be gained in a variety of ways. Mutual customers can reveal competitors' actions or intentions consciously or inadvertently. Trade association meetings and publications are sources of such information. Capital investments in new facilities in new areas or in plant expansions are often revealed by equipment suppliers, banks or real estate brokers and will indicate competitors' product, or market strategies. Mutual suppliers can divulge competitors' inquiries or orders for new and different materials and direct industrial espionage is not unknown.

The business plan for each of the major product families attempts to identify where each product is in its lifecycle—growing, mature, or declining. It is extremely difficult to decide when a product has become obsolete. Particularly when the present management has been responsible for its introduction, there is often extreme reluctance to drop a product from the line if it is still generating some sales revenue. This contrasts dramatically with the first action usually taken by a parent company which acquires another—review each product line to see what items should be dropped from production and do it now.

The steps in business planning are

* Develop accurate data on actual product sales.
* Analyze products for life-cycle position.
* Determine competitors' actions and intentions.
* Prepare specific plans for improving viable products.
* Prepare specific plans for phasing out obsolete ones.

PRODUCTION PLANNING

Production plans are developed simultaneously with business plans but have a shorter horizon (determined by the lead time for changing resources of plant and equipment) and smaller time periods. They attempt to answer the following questions:

* How well are present plant and equipment utilized?
* Where do we have bottlenecks? Excess capacity?
* What total demands will be made on it? When?
* What new technologies will be involved? When?
* What new products will be introduced? When?
* What products will be dropped? When?
* What new plant and equipment will be needed? When?

Production plans are greatly influenced by product life-cycle considerations developed in business plans and must be integrated tightly with them. They must also be integrated closely with strategic plans; the necessity for fast response in the marketplace and flexibility in introducing and manufacturing new products places specific requirements on plant facilities.

Implicit in the development of production plans is the determination of the mission of each facility. Will it be a model shop for prototype development, a department for initial pilot production runs, a proving area for new process technologies or a production facility? How will growth be handled—by expanding the present facility, building new facilities or a combination of both? Will the layout be functional (grouping similar equipment) or line (making families of products)?

Since it deals with the facilities needed, an important consideration in production planning is the identification of components and products which will be purchased from outside sources and those to be manufactured internally. Also important in a multiplant environment is the determination of which components and products will be made in which facilities.

Production planning data are essential in the preparation of the physical capital budget. The quantities and time frames used in the production plans and the questions answered by them will, of course, be much more specific than those in business and strategic planning. The objectives of production planning are

* To determine the resources needed to support the business plans. These include plant, machinery, equipment, materials, people, capital, and the services of outside suppliers.
* To set time tables for the actions of marketing, design engineering, and research and development needed to support the business and production plans.
* To provide summarized data for top management to measure the performance of all the functions in executing the business and production plans.
* To ensure that the resources are applied properly to attain the desired levels of customer service, inventory, profit, and other objectives of the business.

The specific steps required in making a production plan are

* Determine the families to be grouped together.
* Determine the horizon and the time periods to be included in the plan. Many companies make a total plan showing monthly figures for the first year and quarterly data for the second. Data for additional years are usually in half-year or total annual increments. For individual product families, supporting plans are then made in weekly increments for only the first year.
* Set a minimum desired inventory level for products made for stock and a minimum customer order backlog for those produced for specific orders.
* Determine the sales forecast totals for each product family over the planning horizon. These totals will be more accurate than forecasts for specific models.
* Determine the total inventory available at the beginning of the planning period for families of products made for stock and the total customer order backlogs at the beginning of the planning period for families of products built to order.
* Set the desired inventory level and customer order backlog level at the end of the planning period for the corresponding families of products.

* Calculate the total production required for the period. This is the total sales demand plus or minus the difference between beginning and ending inventories or plus or minus the change in total order backlog.
* Spread the total production over the full horizon as desired, considering months with a significant number of holidays, plant vacation shutdowns, lost production during plant expansions or moves, and seasonal products.
* Calculate the total inventory or order backlog at the beginning of each period of the plan. To do this, add (algebraically) the difference between production and shipments for the preceding period to its beginning inventory figure to get the next period's data. For backlogs, use the difference between new orders expected and shipments (equal to production for make-to-order products).

Figure 4–3 is a typical production plan for make-to-stock products; it was made following the procedure just described. It shows on one piece of paper information of great interest to management. This includes projected rates of production, how level or erratic these will be, what rate changes are planned for individual product families, and the totals of production and shipments, all at cost value. As shown in Figure 4–3, net sales income can be added for cash flow determinations.

Additional considerations in making production plans are

* Plans should be made for each manufacturing facility and process which is or could become a bottleneck; they are not needed for all work centers.
* Picking the right measures of capacity to use is important; they should provide the most meaningful possible information to those individuals charged with changing production rates and managing the operations.

Figure 4–3 Typical Production Plan

Month	Jan	Feb	Mar	Oct	Nov	Dec
Family #1 (Units)	55	56	56	52	53	53
Family #2 (Units)	4	5	3	3	4	5
Family #14 (Units)	12	12	12	12	12	12
Repair Parts ($X000)	250	250	250	280	280	280
(All Data $X000) Inventory	1153	1110	1083	991	1058	1104
Production	1038	1074	1037	1015	1048	1037
Shipments at Cost	1081	1101	1121	951	981	991
Net Sales Income	2162	2202	2242	1902	1962	1982

* It is frequently useful to show cumulative sales and production figures instead of detailed figures for each time period. Cumulative data permit comparisons of actual sales and production to the planned figures as time goes on. It would be a mistake to insist that a plant meet a planned increase in production rates if sales in total were not up to the forecast and the inventory was therefore higher than planned. On the other hand, production at the planned rates would be inadequate if sales were exceeding the forecast totals, causing inventories to drop below planned levels. Looking at the three factors—sales, production, and inventory— together in a production plan in aggregate is the best method for executives to get tight control of manufacturing operations.

* Some finite period of time is required for changing production levels and the information on necessary changes must be given to those responsible for making them soon enough to plan for the necessary actions.

* Production plans should not be changed capriciously. Some sets of rules should be established ahead of time indicating when production level changes will be made. Such rules would include inventory being above or below targets by some specified percentage, sales exceeding forecast levels by some specified amount, or production being below or above planned levels by more than a specified tolerance.

Production planning is not a precise procedure nor does it require specific, detailed work standards, although these are the kinds of information many managers believe necessary. Often it is neglected, and this is unfortunate. A sound production plan, even if only rough-cut data are used, can result in good control over flow rates of product families. This is the most important of all production planning information.

The production plan is the basic device for integrating fully the marketing, engineering, production, and finance plans. It provides aggregate information in summarized form making it easier for management to review the performance of the various functions against their individual plans. Its development and use is vital in sound management of manufacturing.

THE PRODUCTION PLAN AND MASTER PRODUCTION SCHEDULE LINKS

Master production schedules and production plans represent two significantly different levels of detail needed in planning manufacturing operations. Production plans are expressed in more general terms and units of measure summarized by groups or families of products. They have a longer horizon than master schedules. The primary use of production plans is in determining limitations in resources which would prevent meeting the output goals so that these limitations can be overcome in time. In the near term, production plans serve as a summary for management of detailed plans driven by master production schedules which must, of course, fit more closely with available resources.

Production plans also reflect top management's policies in inventory management, customer service, and the stability of production as well as in growth rates. They also integrate the more detailed plans of the major functions of the business and as such represent an agreed consensus among top-level functional managers reconciling conflicting policies and strategies.

Master production schedules, on the other hand, are more detailed, apply to specific products or sets of components described by bills of material, and deal with a shorter time frame in more precise time periods. They react to changing product mix and other short-range considerations that are not reflected in the production plan, but they must still be constrained by the overall rates set by the production plan.

MASTER PRODUCTION SCHEDULES

Master production schedules are the most detailed of all the hierarchy of plans. They deal with specifics of bills of material of existing and proposed products and recognize constraints in executing plans. They drive all of the detailed day-to-day operating plans. The name is poor since it connotes order schedule dates and suggests that only production is planned. The term implies that master schedules are part of the execution process. THEY ARE NOT. They attempt to answer the following questions:

What specific products are to be made? How many? When?
What other materials are to be produced? How many? When?
What capacity constraints exist? Our facilities? Suppliers?
What other constraints exist? Tooling? Space? Support staff? Other?

The term "master production schedule" has had different meanings for different people. General agreement has developed among practitioners on a definition which has appeared frequently in the literature and is included in the certification program of the American Production and Inventory Control Society. This is the definition that will be used in this book:

A master schedule is a set of numbers stating what will be made, how many, and when. It is a plan for manufacture, not sales or shipments. It considers the total demands on a plant's resources, including all finished product sales, spare (repair) parts sales, and interplant (affiliate company) needs. It must consider both the capacity of the plant and of its vendors to meet these needs. It provides the overall plan for each manufacturing facility's operation. All detailed planning for materials, people, plant, equipment, and other resources required to manufacture the products will be driven from the master schedule.

A key point to consider is that master production schedules are not "schedules" in the literal sense. Each entry in them consists of a quantity of an item identified by a bill of materials and assigned a time period. Entries are often made to plan for sets of lower-level parts, but no firm commitment needs to be made to produce the parent item. Rather than being a schedule, it should be thought of as a *set of planning numbers*.

Master scheduling is not a part of the execution process. Master schedules should be viewed as *plans to work from, not schedules to work to*. If significant changes become necessary as time passes, master schedules provide a base set of numbers from which to determine quantitatively and specifically what materials and work centers are affected, and to what extent, by the change.

Master production schedules are a matrix for items planned showing the time periods in which each item is to be produced. Weekly time periods are used most often. Occasionally biweekly or monthly periods are used for large, complex products like power generation equipment, ships, and aircraft. Some people more knowledgeable in the power of computers than in the needs of master production scheduling advocate daily time buckets; these are completely impractical, and while they may be more precise, they cannot be more accurate. They enormously multiply the amount of data to be processed and analyzed for no real gain.

Master production schedules are, therefore,

* A planning device, part of the planning hierarchy.
* Statements of what should and can be made.
* A way to balance customers' needs against plant capabilities. Master schedules cannot be wish lists of what a company's management might like to produce. Problems resulting from overstating master schedules are immediate and serious as detailed in Chapter 6.
* A means for management control of the work force, plant, equipment, materials and financing, engineering, and marketing programs.
* A way to coordinate all business functions.
* A basis for measuring performance of each function.

Master production schedules are not

* A collection of sales forecasts.
* A summary of customer orders for products.
* Assembly schedules for detailed production.
* Packaging schedules.
* Part of the execution process.

A typical format for a master production schedule is shown in Figure 4–4. The horizon is six months with one-week time periods. Few companies have the fast-paced operations which need the details provided by

	Month 1				Month 7		
	Weeks				Weeks		
	1	2	3	4	27	28	29
Model 1		15				20	
Model 2	720	720	720	720	720	720	720
Model 3	535	535	535	535	550	550	550
Model 4	35		35		25		25
Model 5		170		170		150	
Family A	310	310	310	310	310	310	310
Total / Month			6685				6690

Figure 4–4 Typical Master Production Schedule

daily time periods; these would use only a few days in the immediate future. Remember that the purpose of planning is to determine the resources needed to support *all of the plans*. The specific results of overloading facilities are detailed in Chapter 5.

A line on the master schedule gives the quantity to be made in each time period of some entity—a finished product, a major subassembly or a planning module—described by a detailed bill of materials and defined by specifications. Similar entities are grouped together with subtotals as shown in Figure 4-4 to match against data in each period of the production plans for the corresponding families. The relations of master production schedules to the other elements of the formal planning system are shown in Chapter 5.

The set of numbers called the master production schedule must be distinguished clearly from master scheduling, the management process by which the numbers are developed. The objectives of master scheduling are

* To provide top management with a means to authorize and control major resources, including capital equipment, worker totals, inventory investment, and cash flow.
* To give management a real handle on customer service and profitability.
* To provide a mechanism to coordinate marketing, production, engineering, and finance activities so that they all work together to achieve common objectives.
* To provide a device to reconcile the needs of customers with the capabilities of manufacturing facilities.

* To provide a means to make more reliable delivery promises to customers and to evaluate the specific effects of changes in delivery schedules.
* To provide an overall measure of how well each major function in the business is able to make a sound plan and then execute it.
* To provide input data to programs developing detailed material, capacity, and financial requirements, thus linking them to the higher-level plans.

Master scheduling is an executive task in which the top-level managers of each major function and the general managers of a company must participate. It develops the formal plans to which the people will work, like the sheet music for a concert orchestra. Harmony in playing the right music will result only when there is teamwork but the major functional groups in manufacturing companies have little in common. Figure 4–5 shows the typical concerns of each of these, highlighting the point that "all-stars" might be a better description of them than "team."

The master scheduling process leading to the development of master production schedules has been used successfully by many firms to develop consensus among these divergent groups on how the company should be run and the roles each will play. The master schedules they produce are then sound bases against which to measure their performance in executing plans.

Figure 4–5

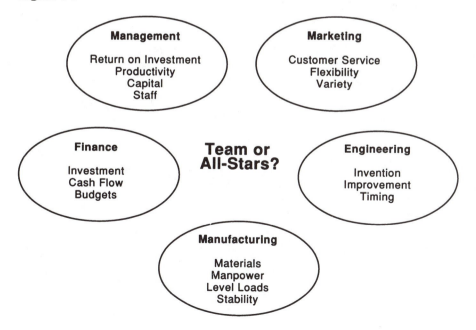

A very pertinent principle should be understood by those participating in the master scheduling process:

9. The validity of any plan increases as its horizon decreases.

The specific reasons this is so and the problems caused by excessively long planning horizons are explained in Chapter 6. The truth of this principle seems self-evident. However, the vital importance of having valid plans has not been clear. In addition, conventional wisdom holds that the replanning capabilities of modern computer-based systems will compensate for poor plans and that cycle times cannot be cut. These views must be changed if manufacturing companies are to achieve top performance and become world class competitors.

MANAGEMENT'S ROLE IN USING THE MASTER PRODUCTION SCHEDULES

Master production schedules drive detailed planning techniques which indicate the proper time to initiate specific actions to procure the necessary resources. The role of top management in using master production schedules includes

* Understanding all of their functions.
* Setting the policies and guidelines needed to direct the detailed actions of those using the plans derived from them.
* Ensuring that they are valid (support higher level plans) and realistic (can be executed).
* Resolving conflicts which inevitably arise among the functions because of their differing concerns.
* Reviewing them regularly and rigorously as their best tool to manage the business details.

Like all complex organisms, manufacturing businesses have well-defined control points. These are found in the four groups of plans in the hierarchy described in this chapter. A detailed discussion of the measures of performance to be used at these control points is found in Chapter 7.

Effective leadership and direction of manufacturing firms requires a working knowledge among top-level executives of these plans, which are literally their "handles on the business," how they are developed, and how they can be used. Like flying airplanes, amateurs at the controls of manufacturing firms are extremely dangerous to themselves and to those nearby.

CHAPTER 5

The System
and Its Role

Systems make it possible, but people make it happen.

SUMMARY

The degree of control possible depends on the complexity of the process, the sophistication of the system, and the character of the environment. Manufacturing, although an extremely complex process, can be controlled using both open- and closed-loop formal systems. Purely automatic control is not yet possible for a total business, but it is in use for many major operations.

There is no best way to control manufacturing. Multiple plants which are parts of a common manufacturing process can be controlled only with integrated systems. The mass of data involved dictates the use of computers and data processing equipment. The system handles data; its role is to provide an integrated set of plans, compare actual execution, and highlight significant deviations. Corrective action requires information, which people must extract from data, analyze, and act on.

Production facilities must make enough in total (have adequate capacity) and work on the right items at the right time (use proper priorities). The core elements of the system to plan both capacities and priorities are known, and all techniques have been developed and tested. Also defined are the required subsystems to process data related to supporting activities internally and in customer and supplier firms. The most heinous crime is to plan for output which exceeds the facilities' capacity.

Computer-based planning and control systems have been a poor investment; expectations have exceeded results. Effective systems require management understanding of the systems' and users' roles and a disciplined, orderly environment. Systems are necessary but not sufficient.

GENERAL CONTROL THEORY

All processes are amenable to some greater or lesser degree of control; manufacturing is no exception. The effectivity (or tightness) of control and the speed of response to changes are a function of the complexity of the process, the sophistication of the control system (hence, its expense and reliability), and the characteristics of the environment, including disciplines, orderliness, and predictability.

Any process in which control is desired must have

* A finite number of interrelated parts interacting in some predictable way to produce desired results.
* Specific plans for the desired results.
* Tolerance ranges for the permissible amount actual results may deviate from plans without correction.
* A minimum time period within which feedback of information on actual performance must occur.
* A maximum time period within which corrective actions are to be taken.

In a purely theoretical engineering sense, control of any process is possible if four elements exist:

* Measurable input
* Measurable output, with a finite goal to be achieved
* A controller, human or mechanical, capable of varying input to influence the process and regulate output
* Feedback providing information on actual performance of the process to be compared to plan

Two types of control systems are available: open loop and closed loop. The former are simpler and less expensive but are incapable of fully automatic control since they require human intervention. Automobile heating and air conditioning controls illustrate the two types. Less expensive cars have open-loop systems, requiring that a person adjust the controls manually to get and keep the desired temperature in the vehicle with changing external conditions. The closed-loop systems in luxury cars require only setting the temperature desired, the control system then adjusts the equipment to maintain it.

The application of control theory to planning and control of manufacturing operations is very complicated. Marketing, sales, design engineering, and production activities are related in very intricate ways. Materials and information in great diversity move through the total process. The effects of changes in any one of many inputs (customer orders, product designs, purchased raw materials, etc.) on the outputs of the total system are not only unclear but also almost impossible to evaluate quantitatively. Many inputs having strong influences on the outputs are external to the business, and, if these problems were not enough, there are many influences on the performance of the total system (e.g., employee motivation) which vary in time over wide ranges. It would seem practically impossible to control manufacturing operations well in such an environment.

The complexity and variability of manufacturing activities and the presence of many unpredictable external forces with direct influence on them preclude the use of automatic systems for full control. Add to these the diversity of management objectives and the varied capabilities of people, and it would seem that no single approach to controlling companies can be applied with any expectation of universal success.

Fully automatic control requiring no human involvement is technically feasible in many quite complex processes. A fine example is flying an airplane, including taking off and landing. Control equipment is now installed in commercial airplanes capable of full operation with no human pilot intervention. High reliability in such systems requires a very carefully controlled environment, however, with stable weather conditions and no collision hazards in the air or on the ground. Redundant system elements ensure against equipment failures. Complex as it is, this has many fewer variables than manufacturing operations.

Fully automatic control is applied successfully also to some manufacturing plants (refineries, for example) and on operations like individual machines, warehouse storage devices and flexible machining cells. Robotics and automation provide automatic controls for improving productivity, quality, and performance of manufacturing operations. However, misapplication of these potentially fine techniques has been counterproductive; the classic example is the experience of General Motors in their 1979–1986 modernization program. It was an expensive failure; the reasons are given in Chapter 6.

Questions arise frequently about the types of systems needed for planning and control of operations involving a number of facilities within a single corporation. Each facility is very conscious of its differences from all others and of its individual needs. Each desires as much autonomy as it can get. These lead management to think separate and different systems are necessary, but they are not. The following principle emphasizes the need for integration of such operations:

10. Manufacturing operations forming parts of a common process are controlled best by an integrated system.

The "parts" referred to in this principle may be a multitude of suppliers, several plants in one company, sister company plants in a large corporation, or many plants located in many countries; the principle applies to all.

Separate, independent systems can be used where plants run independently, procuring and producing all materials needed to serve their own customers. Plants need a common system when they make components for each other, provide only some of the equipment on individual customer orders, serve a common distribution system, or support each other with resources in busy times.

SYSTEM OBJECTIVES

Manufacturing planning and control systems (called the core system here) provide the means to develop fully integrated plans to control the flow of all materials and to provide desired relevant information to people needing it. The system is concerned only with data—numbers, words, and symbols—from which people will extract information. Every physical entity—people, materials, machinery, money—involved in manufacturing must be represented by some number or symbol if it is to be included.

The resulting very large amounts of data relating to even small manufacturing operations dictate the need for modern computers, data collection, and transmission equipment. These make it possible to process data quickly, reliably, and inexpensively to meet the needs of effective planning and control.

The following definitions will apply to three terms used frequently in this book:

> **Planning**—assigning numbers to future events
>
> **Execution**—converting plans to reality
>
> **Control**—measuring deviations from plans of the results of execution, sorting the significant deviations from the trivial, and reporting the former to someone responsible for taking corrective action

All three interact and work together continually in the manufacturing process. The purposes of planning and execution are distinctly different. They are:

Planning—define all of the resources needed to produce *what is planned*
Execution—apply available resources to produce now *what is needed* to meet actual customers' orders

Planning attempts to predict the future while execution focuses on the present situation. Since planning deals with future events, it will never match exactly the later reality of orders received from customers. Even where long-term contracts specify deliveries, there will be design, methods, or other changes which will require differences from what was planned. Shortages of resources must be expected. Ways to minimize such shortages are presented in Chapter 6.

CORE SYSTEM ELEMENTS

Two questions are fundamental in planning and controlling all manufacturing operations: "Are we making enough in total?" and "Are we working on the right items now?" These are commonly referred to as "capacity" and "priority" questions and apply equally to the physical processes and the information processing. Both must be answered "Yes" for manufacturing to be in control.

A primary reason for lack of control in many companies today is neglect of attention to the capacity question and preoccupation with priority. That the opposite emphasis is less harmful is seen in true process plants (i.e., petroleum, chemical, and food processing) where capacity is always the dominant concern.

The core of all planning and control systems is shown in Figure 5–1. This indicates the relationships among the various parts of the planning hierarchy covered in Chapter 4 and the two phases of capacity (right side) and priority (left side) planning and control. The arrows indicate the flow of information among the elements. The arrow bypassing the capacity requirements planning element indicates that rough-cut capacity planning data can and should be used for capacity control.

Figure 5–1 is obviously applicable to any manufacturing business. It illustrates the universal framework stated in principle 3 presented in Chapter 1. A study by the Process Industry Special Interest Group of the American Production and Inventory Control Society developed a framework diagram for the core system needed in their industry (Bibl. 27). This is practically identical to Figure 5–1. It contains the elements common to all manufacturing operations. The activities in strategic, business, and production planning and master production scheduling are presented in detail in Chapter 4.

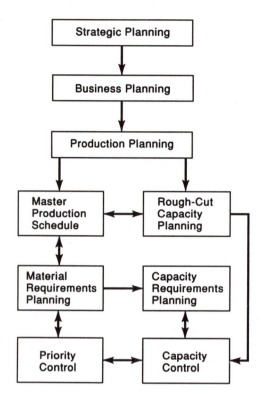

Figure 5–1 Core System Elements

The actual numbers in each element, of course, and even the element's importance in the successful operation of a company, will differ from firm to firm. *Every company's information processing system must contain all elements shown in this framework.*

As stated in Chapter 4, master production schedules are constrained to match the front end of corresponding production plans. They drive material requirements plans and detailed capacity requirements plans for immediate future actions. They also tie directly into detailed plans for other functions.

Rough-cut capacity planning uses data from the front end of the production plan (usually extending farther into the future than master production schedules) to derive aggregate time-phased capacity needs for both plant and supplier facilities. The technique is relatively simple, as illustrated in Figure 5–2.

Data on work hours required in the major work centers to produce a family of products are stored in a bill of labor; a typical one is shown in panel (a) of Figure 5–2. The hours required in each month to produce the total in the production plan of each of the families in each work center is calculated as shown in panel (b). An average of the next two or three months' requirements in each work center is then compared to its recent

(a)

Bill of Labor

Work Center	Standard Hours
110	10
108	8
105	14
104	28

(b)

One Month

Work Centers	Families				Total
Units	#1	#2	#3	#4	
	5570	3120	830	-----	
110	56				
108	45				
105	78				
104	156				
103	50				
101	95				

(c)

Several Months

Work Centers	Present Capacity	Average Month
110	320	330
108	230	200
106	170	150
105	500	650
104	1,500	1,450
103	310	290
102	440	460
101	960	1,010

Figure 5-2 Rough-Cut Capacity Plan

actual output as shown in panel (c) to identify imbalances and initiate corrective actions. This simple yet powerful technique can also be used to play "What if?"—to study the effects of proposed changes in processes, products, or market demands.

This provides a quick, inexpensive way to evaluate the capabilities of present and future facilities to execute the master production schedule. This test of the realism of the plan is essential. A cardinal principle is

11. Plans impossible to execute are the worst kind.

The surest way to guarantee out-of-control performance is to impose on any plant and its suppliers a plan which requires resources which will not be available. Such a plan is impossible to execute. Suppliers and plant work centers with inadequate capacity (commonly called bottlenecks) cannot produce everything needed; the resulting shortages will affect many products, preventing on-time shipments and generating expediting actions. Non-bottleneck centers will produce all materials required by the plan; much of this will not be usable for lack of matching parts. *There is no question of the ultimate effects: poor customer service, high costs, and excessive, unbalanced inventories.*

The validity of the plans is assured only when the sum of the individual products in the master production schedule matches the family requirements in the corresponding periods in the production plan and adequate capacity will be available in all resources to produce the total.

The **material requirements planning** element applies the fundamental logic of manufacturing to priority planning. This logic, presented and discussed in Chapter 1, asks:

* What products are to be manufactured or what services rendered?
* How many are needed?
* When are they needed?
* What resources are required?
* Which of these are available now?
* How many of the others have already been ordered?
* What more is needed? When?

The master production schedules provide specific answers to the first three questions. The manufacturing data base, made up of bills of material, tooling and processing data, machine capability facts, worker information, and financial data define the resources required and available for production. The "When" questions are answered by timephasing all planned data.

A typical material requirements plan is shown in Figure 5–3. The master production schedule calls for making the quantities of some

Master Production Schedule

Week No.	1	2	3	4	5	6	7	8	9
Will Make		20		30		25		35	

Final Assembly Component

Require		20		30		25		35	
Have Now	10								
Will Get		10							
Need				30		25		35	
Start			30		25		35		

Sub Assembly Component

Require				30		25		35	
Have Now									
Will Get				30					
Need						25		35	
Start				25		35			

Purchased Component

Require		10	10	35	10	45	10	10	10	10
Have Now	90									
Will Get										
Need						20	10	10	10	10
Start		100								

Figure 5–3 Typical Material Requirements Plan

product in the periods shown at the top. A bill of materials identifies each component of the final assembly; the plan for one of these is shown. It indicates that 10 units are on hand (have now) and available to meet the first requirement of 20 in period 2 and also that another 10 units are in process (will get) due to be completed in period 2 to meet the balance of the total of 20 needed. The (need) line shows planned orders not yet released which require one period's lead time to process. They should be released (start) one week earlier.

Its bill of materials identifies the parts making up this final assembly component, and Figure 5–3 shows the results of applying to one of them the same logical analysis of materials available and needed. The lowest level in this example is a purchased part with a replenishment order which MRP suggests should be released now. Material requirements planning develops time phased data for all materials linked through bills of material to the item in the master production schedule, recognizing on-hand and on-order quantities.

Detailed capacity requirements planning examines more precisely than the rough-cut technique the loading of specific machines, equipment, and work centers in the very near future. Its objective is to make more effective use of existing resources in scheduling detailed orders through critical operations.

Material and capacity requirements planning are highly precise techniques useful only in the short range future. Projecting these data many weeks into the future is possible with modern computers, *but it is useless*; actual performance will match the plan less and less as the planning horizon gets longer. This is the most powerful argument for short time cycles in priority planning and in execution. Adjusting capacity usually requires long periods to develop skilled workers and to procure machinery and equipment. The compelling need to make a practical capacity requirements plan dictates the use of aggregate data for families of products to ensure the highest possible levels of accuracy. The best that can be obtained is close approximations.

SUBSYSTEMS

In addition to the core planning and control system shown in Figure 4–1, there are many subsystems needed to support related activities. This section will cover only those which feed data directly to the core system or extract data from it in normal operations. Subsystems which interact with these operating systems only indirectly will not be discussed in detail here. These systems include those serving general and administrative management for such purposes as

* Acquisitions, mergers, divestitures—protection against hostile take-overs
* Company/owners relations—quarterly and annual reports and other communications
* Public relations—community affairs, charitable contributions, and environmental concerns
* Legal matters—taxes, licenses, lawsuits
* Capital management—investments, stock management
* Research and development—assuming that their needs for materials and other resources will not be a significant burden on normal operations

Subsystems dealing with **internal company activities** include **product design engineering systems**, such as computer-assisted design (CAD) and computer-assisted engineering (CAE), which should be linked directly to the core system to make readily available to engineers information on active part numbers, common parts, and stocked components to improve standardization and manufacturability. They should transmit electronically new product bills of material, specifications, and engineering changes and maintain the configuration history of each product.

Quality control systems handle data on rejects, scrap, and rework and must be linked directly to the core system to trigger proper corrective actions quickly. Data on process failure to produce good output must be highlighted to workers so that minimum excessive defective materials are produced before the causes are identified and corrected.

Process engineering and selection systems should be linked directly to the core system also. Manufacturing engineers can obtain data on machine and tooling capabilities and loads, can balance operations better, and can evaluate more quickly the effects and potential benefits of automation and robotics. Process changes and time standards can be managed better.

Computer-aided manufacturing (CAM) programs develop instructions for machinery and test equipment. Flexible machining systems (FMS) can process parts automatically. Data on tooling, gauges, test equipment, and other preproduction materials must be available readily to both engineering and production people.

Plant engineering and maintenance systems contain data on plant layout, equipment history (including mean time between failures and preventive maintenance schedules), and inventory of repair and replacement parts for plant machinery. These data are used by manufacturing engineering, planning, and production people in their work and should be readily available. In addition, large savings in utilities costs are possible through careful coordination of operating schedules to avoid excessive peak power loads, waste of power and water, and overloads on waste treatment facilities.

Worker performance systems provide detailed records of actual performance against schedules and specifications in the execution process.

Incentive pay plans and profit sharing require records of people's performance; these all require separate subsystems. Core systems are designed and intended for planning and control activities, not historical record keeping, but tight links of such records with the core system are essential.

Costing systems also need to be linked directly to the core system. Purchased material received and approved for use is the signal to authorize payment of the suppliers' invoices. Product shipments to customers initiate invoicing, and movement of materials to affiliates triggers transfer payments. Actual costs must be accumulated and compared to budgets in the myriad cost centers. The more advanced firms are generating budget figures for inventory, labor, and other costs from detailed operating plans in the core system.

Customer relations require subsystems also. Demand management is the term now covering the planning activities and handling of all types of demand on manufacturing companies from outside sources. These include products and materials furnished to customers, both domestic and foreign, other parent company plants, regional and branch warehouses, subcontractors, suppliers, and consigned stocks in customers' facilities. Materials may be finished products, components, raw materials, and repair parts.

Demand management systems cover communications with customers on their future needs as well as on current orders, forecasting future orders, preparing bids for new contracts or continuation of existing ones, entering and tracking orders and contracts, making delivery promises, and communicating with internal planning functions. Demand management also includes determining the number and location of warehouses together with selecting type and frequency of transportation to and between warehouses and to customers. These activities are commonly called distribution.

The need for careful integration of systems handling demand management and distribution data with the core planning and control system is obvious. Forecasts of future customer demand are major inputs to master production schedule development as are schedules for shipments to branch warehouses. The status of current customer order materials being processed in the plant is vital information to people replying to customer inquiries. Cost data from present operations are needed for preparation of bids on new contracts, and actual costs must be compared with such estimates as work progresses on the contracts won.

When the customer is the U.S. government and its military branches (or prime contractors on such orders), these subsystems become massive and sophisticated in order to comply with the multitude of specifications and auditing regulations. The latest regulations (the so-called Ten Key Standards in FAR 242.7206 Material Management and Accounting Systems) force the integration of operating planning and control and cost accounting systems with severe penalties if not done properly. On-site inspectors and other government representatives demand frequent access to data on current and past activities on contracts.

Invoicing systems bill customers for products shipped to them; these require access to open order files, shipping data, published prices, and contract quotations. Customers' credit status is important information needed by order entry people.

Field service systems covering activities to install and maintain products in customers' facilities need access to data on inventories of replacement products and components. They record the history of product failures and time spent in field work. Such data are used by inventory control, engineering design, and production people together with those invoicing customers.

The number and variety of needs for subsystems is very large but the types of data handled by them are the same in all companies. Clear recognition of this fact will make possible much simpler subsystems and more common ones. This will be very slow in becoming a reality.

Another major set of subsystems handles supplier relations. **Procurement systems** handle activities required in the procurement of goods and services; these subsystems are linked directly to the core planning and control system for data on released and planned supplier orders. They will contain data on the history of suppliers' prices, quality and deliveries, purchase terms and conditions, and information on suppliers' internal operations needed for certification as prime sources. Supplier partnerships now make valuable use of relevant information (union contract expiration dates and other major customers served, for example) influencing the suppliers' reliability as continuing sources. **Supplier rating systems** will produce routine reports of the status of open orders and supplier performance.

Purchase commitment systems are of great use to management producing reports detailing the projected cash needs to pay for materials and services ordered. These systems will be sources of data on prices needed in preparation of bids on new contracts or estimates of costs of new products.

Procurement subsystems must be linked closely with quality control, receiving, and accounts payable subsystems authorizing and tracking payment of suppliers for materials and services delivered. It is obvious that they must tie closely to the core system to keep them both locked in step.

REQUIREMENTS FOR EFFECTIVE SYSTEMS

American management has spent too much money on computer systems that allow them to do the wrong things faster. My experiences with many client companies has convinced me that the return on the billions of dollars invested in information systems in industry has been abysmally low because

* Managers think that systems solve existing problems. They do not; they add new problems.
* Managers believe that they can buy their way out of trouble with expensive systems. They cannot; they must work their way out.
* Inadequate efforts are made to get people ready for system implementation. Education is the greatest need.
* The needs of the business for systems have been poorly defined and inadequate specifications written.
* The roles of formal systems and the people using them are not clearly understood. Systems process data; people make decisions and take action using information extracted from data.

No system, manual or computer based, simple or sophisticated, can be expected to work well in an unpredictable environment. When the methods discussed in Chapter 6 are applied diligently and are working effectively to reduce chaos in the manufacturing environment, it will then be feasible to implement a total system. To do this it is necessary to take several very critical steps which had better not be left to neophytes or amateurs:

* Define the core and subsystems needed for the total manufacturing business.
* Determine the elements of each which are critical for good control.
* Design the data base and files to be used.
* Select the performance measures to be used in each and establish tolerances for acceptable performance.
* Synthesize a network of these systems which can be operated to achieve control of the total process.

Such a network is called computer integrated manufacturing (CIM). Ultimately, the network will link all computer programs used in every department of a company which transmit or receive data flowing between systems. All data need not flow to other systems; some are used only internally in one area. The key to designing practical networks is to make data available to those who need it but to no others. Careful definition of the proper activities and primary tasks of each organizational group is a prerequisite for sound network design.

Well-designed, complete, and fully integrated systems are necessary for tight control, but they are not sufficient. Systems simply process data, efficiently and at blinding speeds. People must separate out the information they need and use it well.

CHAPTER 6

Effective Execution and Control

Making enough in total is a prerequisite to making all of the right things.

SUMMARY

The first job of manufacturing management is getting its own house in order. This provides a stronger base to cope with external influences. The essence of control is qualified people making sound plans, executed in a disciplined environment. There are three requirements: first, make sound plans; second, measure actual performance accurately and timely, and third, compare with plans, identify significant deviations, and report them to those responsible for corrective action. The speed of response determines the benefits achieved.

Improving internal control requires eliminating unnecessary activities, balancing sequences of operations, attacking all causes of delays, and speeding up all activities. Suppliers, customers, and all company people should be enlisted.

Achieving excellence causes culture shock— developing a new way of life for everyone. People's perspective of the business and the roles of everyone in it will be radically changed. These changes cannot be achieved with fads, gimmicks, or buzzwords. Most dramatic will be the change in roles of staff experts—quality control, manufacturing engineering, planning and control, and maintenance—from doers to teachers. Most of their actions will be taught to production workers.

Improvement can be made in all groups simultaneously. Failure to accept this, undertake the necessary education, and provide strong motivation will result in failure to compete.

REQUIREMENTS FOR CONTROL

External factors beyond an individual company's control may interfere with, even preclude, its being a strong competitor. It is always true, however, that using these as excuses for doing nothing internally guarantees failure. In the majority of companies, the damaging effects of external influences could be greatly reduced and sometimes eliminated if internal operations were under better control. The calls for government protection against unfair foreign trade practices illustrate this clearly. Superior performance in delivering better products is fundamental to penetration of any market. Japanese markets are closed to many U.S. products because these products are not competitive, even in U.S. markets.

Getting its own house in better order must be the first concern of management; it is here that their ability to effect improvements is greatest. In addition, without this improvement in internal operations, efforts to cope with external influences will be handicapped at best and hamstrung at worst.

The advent of powerful computers and the development of the theory and practice of planning and control make greatly improved control possible. Having even very sophisticated systems in operation, however, is not enough to make it happen.

The essence of control is qualified people making sound plans and executing them in an orderly, predictable environment. Qualified people understand their primary jobs and give them priority attention. To do these jobs effectively, they need information which they extract from the system. They must know where the system gets the data it uses, how it processes these data, and the timing and tolerances built into it. They should know how much latitude they can exercise in acting on the information and have a strong sense of urgency for acting quickly.

Control requires information; systems generate data. The difference is in the usefulness of the data and in the depth of understanding of its true meaning by those reading the data. Swamped with data while starved for information describes many people in manufacturing businesses using computers. They are the victims when they have no control over which data are produced and how they are processed; they are the culprits when they have such control but do not give careful attention to collection, processing, and reporting the proper data.

There are six requirements for tight, effective control; these are listed in Figure 6–1. All six are necessary. While they are easily stated, they are not easy to get.

Valid Plans

Figure 6-1 Requirements for Control

Timely Feedback

Preset Tolerances

Exception Reports

Thorough Review

Prompt Action

Valid Plans

As defined in Chapter 5, planning is the process of assigning numbers to future activities expected or desired to occur. Sound plans recognize that no prediction of the future is likely to be accurate; changes are inevitable. They will identify possible alternative courses of action and will include contingency plans to take advantage of opportunities or minimize the problems resulting from planning errors. Planning data are "soft" approximations unlike execution data, which are "hard" realities.

Sound plans have four characteristics:

*   They integrate the actions of all functions.
*   They are supported by adequate resources.
*   They have accurate data.
*   They have the shortest possible horizons.

The considerable effort and expense of formal planning and control should be made only in support of the primary activities of groups and individuals. Planning is too important and too expensive to waste it on trivia. Subordinate work needs some planning also, of course; this should be done informally by the individuals involved. All formal plans must be tightly integrated to coordinate the activities of the various people engaged in the manufacturing process.

The fundamental question, "Are we making enough in total?" is more important than, "Are we working on the right items today?" although the latter receives far more attention. As emphasized in Chapter 5, capacity planning is vital to define the resources needed to support the plans. Nothing is more destructive of good performance than inadequate resources.

Accuracy of data is equally important. Effective control is impossible using erroneous information. At best it will cause inappropriate responses; at worst, the formal system will be ignored. Although not widely recognized, eliminating errors from vital records is quick, inexpensive, practical, and effective. In addition, it is a fine profit-improvement program. Additional information on this is found in Chapter 7 and (Bibl. 15).

The importance of fast, smooth flow and short lead times is a major topic in this book. The basic need for valid plans is the principal reason for this, but there are many serious and costly problems that result from long planning horizons. These are indicated in Figure 6–2. Most of these are self-evident but the magnitude of the effects is difficult to understand. *Modern developments in improved operations planning and control are often counterintuitive.* It is almost impossible for someone lacking a sound understanding of how manufacturing works to believe that such large benefits can result in so many activities from simply reducing cycle times.

Invalid Plans   **Figure 6–2 Long-Cycle Problems**

Too Many Crises

Poor Supplier Deliveries

Unbalanced Inventories

High Obsolescence Losses

Excessive Overhead Costs

Oversized Plants

Inflexible Operations

Timely Feedback

Planning is followed by execution; actions are taken to convert plans to reality. The two occur simultaneously over the planning horizon. By feeding data on actual performance into the planning system, execution can be compared to plans and significant deviations can be highlighted.

Timeliness is essential for tight control. Information must be made available soon after beginning execution of plans, while deviations are still small enough for fast correction. Weekly reports of activities will be too late for fast-paced operations requiring quick corrective actions; they will be too frequent for other slower-paced businesses. Real-time, on-line data collection systems are rarely required except for fully automatic operations. Managers must set the proper frequency of control reports for their functions.

Preset Tolerances

Good plans will include estimates of how wrong projections might be. Such estimates will be expressed in a tolerance range for planned data determined by striking a workable balance between tightness of control desired and that achievable in the process. Those responsible for corrective action must set tolerance ranges defining acceptable limits on deviations from each plan so that exception reports can be made.

Exception Reports

Focusing attention on the important items needing immediate action requires separating significant deviations from minor variations from plan. The latter are often unavoidable and should be ignored; efforts to correct them will be wasted and, even worse, will dilute efforts on major ones. Systems should be designed to ignore variances within tolerance and highlight only those requiring action. If problems are numerous, there may be too many exceptions reported for proper attention and handling. The only sound recourse is to open up tolerances on selected items to reduce the number of exceptions.

Thorough Review

The first look at a variance from plan leads underqualified people to the wrong conclusion about the real problem causing it. The symptoms often hide the disease. Capacity problems show up as bad priorities and priority problems result in apparently overloaded facilities. An in-depth review by a qualified individual is needed to identify the proper corrective action for each item on exception reports.

Prompt Action

The speed of response to signals from the system on items outside control tolerances will determine the benefits achieved. The slower the response, the greater will be the deviation, the time for and the expense of corrective actions. Two types of response are possible:

* Get back on plan.
* Change the plan.

Replanning with modern computer-based systems is fast and all too easy. It is possible, although rarely desirable, to replan in real time, every minute on the minute. Weekly replanning is adequate for practically all manufacturing operations. Some continuous flow and process plants may require more frequent review of operating plans if they serve really dynamic markets. The following principle will require basic changes in the attitudes of many managers who believe fast replanning is a benefit:

12. Replanning is the last resort; first get back on plan.

As long as plans are still valid, replanning should be avoided and extra efforts exerted to get back on plan. Replanning is acceptance of failure of execution unless it is required by events beyond control. It is capable of generating a flood of changes in detailed plans and schedules; these have caused unnecessary nervous prostration in too many firms.

IMPROVING INTERNAL CONTROL

Fundamental to improving internal control are five activities whose basic objectives are to reduce both the complexity and unpredictability of the manufacturing process:

* Eliminating all unnecessary activities. It is senseless to improve the efficiency of doing anything that can be avoided completely. The first test before robotics and automation are employed is, "Can this operation be eliminated?"
* Balance all sequences of activities involving either information or material flows. This may require lower utilization or less efficient use of some facilities but these losses will be small when compared to the overall gains.
* Attack all problems causing disruption or delay. No activities or areas should be exempt. No problem should be considered unsolvable. Effective execution requires solving, not covering up, problems by good teamwork and fast corrective action.
* Speed up all activities. Time is the most precious of all manufacturing resources.
* Enlist all customers, suppliers, and company people in the improvement process.

These are being carried out successfully in so many companies in so many different industries that it has become obvious that the methods are universally applicable to all types of manufacturing.

Eliminating unnecessary activities is accepted readily as a legitimate and worthwhile goal. The difficulty encountered in doing it lies in the definition of "unnecessary." One department believes sincerely that it is necessary to inspect and correct the information or materials fed to them by another group. Until the feeder department ceases delivering "defects," finding and fixing them will seem "necessary" to the users.

Even more difficult to rate unnecessary are activities which can be eliminated only by the concerted actions of many groups. Material handling, storerooms, and incoming inspection are classic examples. Difficult as it may be, it is very worthwhile to work on eliminating them. *Ending unneeded activities will generate much larger benefits than improving needed ones.*

The technique which is proving effective is to get everyone working on small teams assigned to achieving defined objectives in their own and related work areas. Management specifies what to do and the people decide how to do it—and then get it done!

Developing new flowline plant layout, improving inventory control, and getting certified suppliers take time and the efforts of many people. If not promoted and supported strongly by management, however, actions will be delayed a long time while many unnecessary and very expensive activities continue.

Like attacking unnecessary activities, balancing sequences of activities is more a perceptual than a technical problem. All manufacturing plants, regardless of how batch oriented they may appear, have many sequences of operations which involve a flow of similar information or materials through similar processes. When these are identified, it is an easy step to integrate them into a closely knit, balanced operation. The key is identifying groups of similar (not necessarily identical) items receiving similar (not identical) treatment and integrating the processing.

Shorter time and smoother flow are permanent partners. The process and repetitive manufacturers think "flow" of materials is natural; the word is rarely used by batch processors and never by job shop and aerospace/defense people; they think that it is not applicable. A better term, perhaps, is "move"; this is clearly applicable to all types of production. In order to get materials and information moving more steadily, of course, the operations and activities through which they pass must be balanced better. This is an axiom of the theory of manufacturing control and is also universally applicable.

Balanced operations are those which process the same total amount of work in a given time period. Their throughputs (the actual amounts of work handled) are the same although their capacities (their abilities to handle work) may differ. Lack of balance results in some idle time of machines or people and/or in excess work-in-process. *It is not true that idle time is a more serious or costly problem than excess work-in-process*; the latter results in longer manufacturing cycle times which carry many serious side effects. Bottlenecks, operations having inadequate capacity to handle required throughputs, however, are much more serious than either idle time or excess work-in-process because they jeopardize the validity of the whole operating plan.

Control of balance is achieved only by control of work input to and output from operations. The total of work released to or received by an operation (input) and the amount of work turned out by operations (output) must be controlled tightly before the priorities of individual orders can be managed properly. The relevant principle is:

13. Making enough in total is a prerequisite of making the right things.

Balance is needed for both information and material flows throughout the total manufacturing process involving a company, its customers, and its suppliers in one linked sequence. Input to each segment and its throughput providing input to the next, can be buffered only by paperwork files and by inventories. Both add time to processing cycles and, for this reason alone, are undesirable; they add considerable costs also.

Balance can always be improved by

* Reducing the batch, lot, or order quantities. This requires cutting setup times, believed by many managers and others to be expensive and time consuming and often impossible. This is just another myth of manufacturing.
* Arranging machines into cells, called variously group technology, flexible machining systems, or flowlines. This may involve lower machine utilization but will usually result in higher overall benefits.
* Altering processing sequences and/or operations on individual batches. In this approach, each production lot of individual items is studied to rearrange operation sequences or times for the best balance. As with flowline layout, there may be some penalties but these will be exceeded by the benefits.
* Changing processing sequences among several batches using computer simulations to study alternatives. Mathematical techniques to optimize schedules of several orders moving through various sequences of operations are well known and widely used.

Almost every problem encountered in manufacturing will cause disruption and delays in flows of information or material. This suggests that monitoring the flows is the simplest method of getting early warnings of active problems. As early as 1965, I used a technique called "Flow Control" (Bibl. 18) to detect work stalled in work centers beyond an allowable time. This was simpler, cheaper, and more effective than expensive scheduling and tracking of all work orders. Following detection of delays, finding root causes, and fixing them promptly requires well-trained teams of highly motivated people.

Speeding up the flows of information and materials will occur in two phases:

* Elimination of unneeded "fat," cushions of work which will not be missed.
* Further reduction of paperwork and material queues which could result in starving operations.

A chart like Figure 6–3 can be drawn easily for important sequences of activities for whole plants or for product families. Paperwork and production processes can both be studied. Precision is not required; estimates of the length of time paperwork and materials sit in office, plant, and storage areas are sufficient. The wider vertical bars show the best opportunities for cutting time from the cycle. These, however, may not be the easiest to reduce and the latter should be attacked first. Sampling the actual queues of work will quickly reveal excesses which can be removed immediately without potentially harmful side effects.

More study and work is required to smooth out flows so that queues of work-in-process can be reduced further. The goal is clear: nothing waits. Only in continuous processing (as in petroleum refineries and chemical plants) will this goal be realized fully. Every plant can move toward it, of course, and how close many have gotten is very surprising. Frank Gue covers the techniques for accomplishing this in his excellent book on control of work-in-process (Bibl. 8).

Figure 6–3 Production Cycle Time

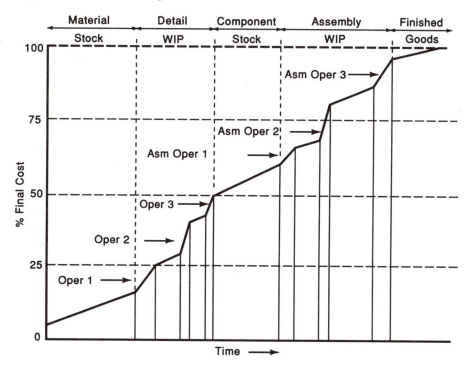

Every company has myriad problems causing delays and interruptions. No company can afford to hire a staff of experts to attack and solve them all. They must use their own people who will need training, opportunity, and motivation to get the job done. Teams of such people are now performing what their management considers miracles in many well-run companies.

Working within their own departments, such teams are able to make excellent progress. When they have their own house in order, even greater progress is possible through attacking the problems one department may cause another or revising the way one works to improve operations in another. Interdepartmental improvements will reveal many activities which can be combined or eliminated to generate large benefits.

Likewise, intercompany studies undertaken with customers and suppliers are extremely productive of improvements. One well-known "secret" of Japanese success is the very close relations they establish and maintain with customers and suppliers. This has been proven to work in the United States also in spite of skeptics' doubts and the reasons they cited why it wouldn't. Cultural differences, antagonistic labor unions, antitrust laws, and even management's preoccupation with short-term profits are no real barriers to achieving such cooperation.

Effective execution and control is possible in every manufacturing company. This does not imply that it will be easy to achieve in any firm; it will not. The requirements are clearly defined. The needed techniques are available and tested. Systems to integrate the planning and control efforts are also known and tested. These are the technical elements in the situation, however, and they will neither make nor break the programs needed to improve the competitive performance of companies.

CULTURAL CHANGES NEEDED

Success in any company will be determined by the ability of its managers to change the culture of their people. Of all the activities involved in making companies world-class competitors, none is as important as this. Only through education, training, motivation, and leadership will people change their ways of life as needed to make success possible.

Running manufacturing the way it ought to be run requires fundamental changes in most companies. Every organizational group must be involved. Their objectives, their relations to others and their role in the total business process—literally, their ways of life—must be changed. The goal of the changes is to smooth out and speed up the process of satisfying customers, earning adequate profits, and employing capital effectively. The extent of the changes will be to alter everyone's perception of the business and the roles of all people in it.

Heavy publicity has been given to potentially large gains in productivity, inventory reductions, and cuts in costs through use of manufacturing resources planning (MRPII) systems, just-in-time strategies, flexible machining systems, and total quality control programs. These and other buzzwords have caught the eyes of many managers hoping for a quick fix of serious problems. A U.S. company whose costs were 35% above those of their foreign competitor, mounted a massive (and expensive) effort to improve plant operations—and made excellent progress. They were appalled to find that they were now 40% higher in cost. The other firm had improved its designs for manufacturability, not only offsetting the U.S. firm's cost reductions but increasing its own cost advantage.

All functions of a company must be improved to ensure its survival, just as all parts of a human's body must be healthy if it is to be fully productive throughout a normal life span. This principle applies:

14. Improvements can and should be made in all functions simultaneously.

It is a gross error to work on only one at a time. If operations are poorly planned and controlled, this must be corrected but the potential improvement will be limited by many constraints like

* Poor market strategy and lack of knowledge of customers' needs.
* Inept advertising and selling.
* Inferior product designs.
* Adversarial supplier relationships.
* Lack of teamwork among organizational functio.ıs.
* Underqualified people.

Getting teamwork among the major functions of engineering, marketing, sales, production, and finance is difficult; each has its own concepts of the company's needs (see Figure 4–5 and the discussion in Chapter 4). Top-level managers will agree readily that profits are a vital factor in the firm's success and even on some desirable increase. Ask each what three actions are most important in achieving these profits, however, and agreement vanishes. Engineering will suggest the application of new technologies to product design, tighter tolerances in the plant's adherence to specifications, and more time for design work. Marketing and sales will say quicker, more on-time deliveries, more varieties of products, faster introduction of new models, and lower costs. Production will want fewer models, less frequent engineering changes, and higher selling prices. Finance will ask for tighter adherence to budgets, higher inventory turnover, and better labor efficiency and machine utilization. Teamwork? What's that? Each thinks the others are bigger culprits.

These narrow views are fostered by long time U.S. practices of specialization and promotion from within functions. Certainly, the head of each function must be strong, technically capable and concerned with its goals and objectives. To be an effective member of a management team, however, each must have an adequate understanding of the other functions. Rotational assignments of managers to functions other than their specialization are being used by many companies to achieve this and have been practiced for a long time in Japan.

Top Management

Top-level executives are not exempted from cultural changes; in fact, their cultural revolution may be more important than that of most others in their organization. They must learn

* That just knowing how to read financial reports is not enough to achieve manufacturing excellence.
* How the manufacturing process really works so that they know how to use it to achieve corporate goals.
* The dangers of arbitrary edicts.
* The primary roles of each organizational group and how to get these to function well together as a team.
* How to use their formal systems to get the facts they need to make decisions, not depending on data from independent side records and unsupported opinions.
* The penalties incurred by having inadequate capacity in plant and suppliers' facilities to produce the total output desired.

The following principle, repeated from Chapter 5, is applicable here also:

11. Plans impossible to execute are the worst kind.

No other mistake in manufacturing incurs such severe penalties. All of the firm's major objectives are adversely affected; poorer customer service, bad-quality products, and lower return on investment will be inevitable. Crises will dictate actions and will affect performance adversely throughout the business. While these effects are obvious and the logical result of inadequate capacity, this is still the most common problem of industry.

Marketing strategies to attract more customers are always important top management concerns; they must see clearly that plant capital investment to ensure adequate capacity is at least as important. Management is a game of making the least worst choices; impossible as it may be for most executives to conceive, delaying, or even turning down, a customer's order which overloads a plant may be the lesser of the evils, by far.

An awareness of the importance of time is paramount in top management decisions and actions. Competition in world markets is demanding much faster response to more rapidly changing needs. Every action influencing the flows of information and materials must be scrutinized continuously to make them smoother and faster. Continuous efforts to shorten processing times and eliminate delays must become a way of life, not a sometime program. Progress can be made steadily and surely in any company; in some it can be spectacular. The most effective executives will be those who combine patience and perseverance, an unusual combination, in demanding and fostering constant improvements in speed and flexibility of all activities.

Finance and Accounting

Business schools in major universities have promoted very successfully among their MBA candidates the notion that managers do not have to know the business, all they need to know is how to read the numbers in the financial reports. Chapter 2 contains a discussion of this fallacy and about its effects on financial manipulations involving takeovers, acquisitions, mergers, and divestitures. These have been responsible for creating and exacerbating many problems which have contributed to the loss in competitive position of American manufacturing companies. These problems include overemphasizing short-term profits, diverting capital from applications-enhancing manufacturing (i.e., research and development, adding capacity, educating employees), distraction of executives from directing operations to initiating or fighting mergers and acquisitions, and failing to take corrective actions to salvage troubled firms.

The financial view of manufacturing treats individual plants or companies within a corporation as if they were stocks and bonds in a portfolio. If earnings per share or return on assets is not high enough, it appears that the business should be sold. The fallacy of this is not realizing that the business could be managed better to produce adequate earnings. The tragedy is that we are surrendering U.S. technology, markets, standard of living, and jobs to foreign competitors in the mistaken belief that factors beyond our control prevent our being competitive.

The thesis of "managing by the numbers" assumes that all needed numbers are available, that they are correct and that intangible factors are, at best, secondary. All three are patently false assumptions. All numbers relevant to a decision are rarely available. More than half the factors involved in a decision of whether to increase capacity by using overtime or hiring more people, subcontracting work, or buying new equipment, cannot be found in financial records. Financial and cost data may appear highly precise, but their sources and calculation methods make their accuracy very dubious. Important numbers like the cost of carrying inventory are guesses.

While cost data are typically poor, those for the values of resources are far worse and often nonexistent. Book values of machines bear no relation to useful value or economic life. The value of unused capacity is intangible although machine utilization can be calculated to precise percentages. A pure-numbers manager will give more importance to increasing utilization rates than to having spare capacity. Business-wise managers seeing new opportunities to serve more customers better will opt for unused capacity to take advantage of them. The loss of market share by U.S. machine tool makers shows the deadly effects of decision making by numbers alone without understanding what they mean.

The analysis needed to make the decision of whether or not to implement a CAD/CAM system has some tangible factors. Unfortunately, you can't make a good decision on these alone; the real value will be far greater than the drafting hours saved or the number of drawings eliminated. Important factors like the value of speeding up designs, increasing standardization of components, and avoiding human errors cannot be quantified using conventional cost accounting systems data.

Accounting systems in the past have been designed and have functioned well to serve the needs of company executives and outsiders interested in a company's past performance. They are called, properly, financial accounting systems. Their focus has been on the past; recording history and keeping score is a good description of what they do best.

When called upon to provide information for operating managers, however, such systems need modification; future events must be handled as well as recording past activities. In every company some formal plans and budgets are developed and computers applied in many of them to process the data.

However, too little thought is given to the requirements for control—sound plans, timely feedback of actual performance against plans, highlighting important deviations, and reporting promptly to individuals responsible for corrective actions. As a result, managers struggle through stacks of data searching for needles of information. Financial accounting systems developed for the scorekeepers cannot meet the needs of the players in the game of manufacturing.

In establishing priorities between getting better accounting systems and improving business systems, the principle is

15. Learn to play a better game, not just keep a better score.

Many numbers are needed for planning and control, but these must be *numbers representing things that really count, not just those easily counted.* The emphasis must be shifted from masses of precise data on past results to the important few numbers for better decision making. Chapter 7 has more coverage of the deficiencies of financial accounting systems and specific information on the most useful measures of performance.

Current accounting systems are inadequate in all departments for assisting operations managers in improving performance . New control systems are needed for these decision makers. The cultural change needed among financial people attempting to serve the needs of operating managers is realizing that *accuracy is preferable to precision and relevancy is better than consistency.*

Marketing and Sales

As vitally needed is a clear vision of the primary role of marketing and sales—providing intelligence (information) about the marketplace of their customers. Garnering information about customers' future needs must be viewed as at least as important as getting an order. Such data can be translated into better forecasts, earlier warning signals of changing trends, better product designs, and improved deliveries, all of which lead to better customer relations. There is a major difference between serving the needs of customers and catering to their wants; one is managing sales, the other is order taking.

Arm's-length relationships between customers and suppliers, coupled with poor delivery performance by the latter, has resulted in distorted communications. Customers "pad" their orders and specify earlier-than-needed delivery just in case the materials ordered are of poor quality or are late. They refuse to make long-term commitments, reserving the right to switch to another supplier, or they split their orders among several suppliers.

Poor communications lead to poor performance in a vicious cycle. This has characterized procurement in the past. To break out of this, the guiding principle is

16. Know customers' real needs, not just their wants.

Customers' orders express their wants; these are often quite different from their real needs, particularly in delivery dates. Suppliers also need information on customers' aggregate needs—long-term totals of families of similar items—for capacity planning. They also need to know the specific mix of items to be ordered in the near future for priority control. Few marketing and sales people recognize that providing a clear picture of their customers' true needs is one of their most important tasks.

Marketing must play an active role also in master scheduling (covered in Chapter 4), participating in the development and maintenance of the master production schedule. Steady pressure is needed on weeding out unnecessary products as well as adding useful ones; the latter is common practice, but the former is a random exercise lacking enthusiasm. Both activities have major effects on customers' and internal operations and must include marketing and sales participation. Both will be handled more constructively if marketing and sales people have a basic understanding of how manufacturing planning, control, and execution work in operations.

Delivery promises to customers will be reliable only when they are based on valid master production schedules. "Formulas" and "standard" delivery times for product families cannot work because they ignore the total loads generated by all orders in any period. When the plant is behind schedule and cannot produce everything wanted, marketing and sales have a deep interest in and must participate in making the difficult decision of which customers' orders will be delayed. This is an important part of the process called master scheduling.

Warehousing and Distribution

Marketing and sales people believe strongly that more warehouses lead directly to increased sales. Field warehouses are intended to get products closer to customers. Sometimes they provide a real competitive advantage but often are unnecessary. "Closer" means time rather than distance and modern distribution methods have shrunk the world. Low airfreight costs, dedicated truck service, and fast highways move materials at very high speeds. If production is fast and flexible, many goods can be brought to customers without an intermediate stop in warehouses. Techniques for improving warehouse operations are included in an appendix in my *Principles and Techniques* book (Bibl. 18).

Nonmarketing managers usually view regional and branch warehouses as necessary evils. They are more often cost centers than profit centers. Costs of operation are significant and large amounts of capital are tied up in inventories; few warehouses achieve the 50 to 60 inventory turns possible.

When served by well-run plants and properly located, field warehouses can be a cost-effective, competitive advantage. When I took over their management, freight costs moving goods to warehouses from my two steel-strapping plants (and between warehouses to rebalance inventories frequently) exceeded direct labor costs to produce the strapping and tools. Studies showed that we really needed only 6 of the 14 warehouses we had, and we gave better service to customers with the smaller number.

The justification of warehouses must be more rigorous. It must include specific discussions with customers as well as investigations of alternate means of getting products quickly to them. When warehouses are deemed necessary, the following actions will minimize inventory and costs:

* Include warehouse requirements and inventory changes in plant capacity planning. The importance of capacity being adequate requires attention to all significant demands on plant facilities, including warehouses.
* Determine the economical replenishment period for each warehouse. This ensures economical freight lots and regular shipping frequencies.
* Control warehouse inventories from one central office; don't permit independent ordering.
* Set target levels for each item to achieve desired customer service levels and inventory turns; order up to the targets in each replenishment period.
* Use customer order entry data, not warehouse shipments, in determining replenishment quantities.
* Concentrate reserves (safety stocks) in only a very few locations, preferably the supplying plants.
* Keep distribution and warehouse people fully advised of material availability everywhere. Demand teamwork to get the best service with the least cost and capital investment.

Design Engineering

Three factors have combined to require fundamental changes in the way products are invented and improved: demand by customers for more varieties of products, increasingly fast response by competitors in getting new products to market, and clear recognition of the influence of design and later changes in design on costs and operations. No company can survive today by offering a limited line of product models. Gone are the days when such a market strategy could work by ensuring high volumes and low production costs. It has been proven that low volumes are no excuse for high costs.

Taking years to develop new car models has cut deeply into the market share of U.S. automobile manufacturers whose competitors do it in months. An extra few months of delay in bringing any new product to market can cost 50% or more of total potential profits and can limit market share permanently if competitors move more quickly. Too often it takes longer to design products (and debug design faults) than to buy materials and make them. The successful company with a future will be *faster than competitors getting to market with soundly designed products* embodying new technologies and meeting new desires of customers.

Few product design engineers understand the influences their work has on subsequent planning and production. Little has been published to acquaint them with these phases of manufacturing; an exception is my son Keith's fine book (Bibl. 22). From 60% to 90% of factory costs of products are fixed once the design has been firmed up and released for production. Most expensive processing operations are also determined by the design. Many types of overhead costs—tooling, scrap, rework, procuring and storing materials, record keeping—are locked in at high levels by designs which are difficult to manufacture.

Few engineering managers, and even fewer design engineers, have a broad view of how a manufacturing business operates and how much their activities affect the rest of the organization. They are preoccupied with the technical functioning of products and disinterested in manufacturing operations. They must be made to understand this principle:

17. Sound design means much more than proper functioning.

Design engineering responsibility must extend beyond the proper functioning of products. *They have more impact on competitiveness than any other organizational group.* Manufacturability is equally as important as function. *Business Week*, in its November 20, 1989 "Science & Technology" section told the story of Ford's new modular engine design. Its characteristics were

* Modular construction based on an efficient combustion chamber easily convertible to V-6 or V-8 and adaptable to model changes to meet shifting customer desires.
* Simplified design achieving 25% reduction in parts by eliminating accessory brackets and other components.
* More common parts (about 350) among different models.
* Flexible machining to use cast iron (basic) and aluminum (high-performance) engine blocks in several model families, produce small runs with rapid changeover of models, and permit shifting quickly to smaller, lighter engines if government fuel economy standards require this.

This is a classic example of designing for manufacturability and for flexibility to meet changing market strategies.

Design engineers cannot work independently; the needs of those concerned with component production, assembly, testing, packaging, field service, and furnishing spare parts must be met during, not after, the design phase. Teamwork means developing design details together, not passing the design along like a baton in a relay race. *Business Week*'s April 30, 1990 issue contained a special report titled, "A Smarter Way to Manufacture," which highlighted the importance of "CE," a recent addition to our acronyms meaning concurrect engineering. Featured were a team of NCR people, including designers, processing, production, purchasing and field service, who developed a new product in half the normal time, with 85% fewer parts and one-fourth the assembly labor. The synergism of such teams has been proved often.

The uses by others of information supplied with designs must also become an engineer's concern. Part numbers are necessary to provide unique names (but not descriptions) for things vitally required to make products. These things, in addition to component parts, include tooling, fixtures, gauges, test equipment, and spare parts for plant equipment and machinery. Bills of material are frameworks on which much planning is hung; the way they are structured is vital to planning and control, production, and cost accounting, as well as design.

Simplicity and standardization are also as necessary as proper functioning of products. In these times of high technology and rapid change, this is often challenged. "How can a product be simple and do all these complex things?" is heard frequently from design engineers. The answer is, "Unless it is simple, it won't work well and we can't build it right." Who can forget Rube Goldberg's ingenious mechanisms? Who could ever make them work?

Standardization seems to connote hamstringing creativity, and this is often the effect of establishing standards. The key concept is, "Today's best is tomorrow's standard." Standards must change as often as better ways are developed. They are intended to convey to all concerned the best methods, materials, techniques, and ways of doing things today, recognizing that someone will find better ways tomorrow and these will then be the standard.

Manufacturing Engineering

Manufacturing engineering (also called industrial and process engineering) made enormous contributions to improving productivity in the early decades of the industrial revolution. When operations were disorganized, unstructured, and subject to changing whims of individuals, developing and applying "standard" methods and times repaid the costs incurred many times over.

This is no longer true. Serious problems now cause costs to exceed benefits. The rigorous imposition of standards and lack of adequate rewards stifled the initiative of workers to reveal their ideas for improvements. Attempts to enforce standards brought adversarial relations between labor and management. Accelerating rates of change in products and processes escalated the cost of keeping standards current. *Establishment of detailed time standards on production operations is now well past the point of diminishing returns in most companies.*

Even more important, the recognition of the benefits of smooth fast flow of materials through all operations provides a more fertile field for use of good manufacturing engineers, a very scarce resource. An appropriate principle is

18. Setting time standards is secondary to smoothing and speeding flow.

Instead of working in offices developing precise standards, getting engineers out in the plant working with production people to smooth and speed the flow of materials results in order of magnitude higher benefits. Shortening setups, for example, will reduce many more costs and improve the plant's performance far more than the same effort spent setting new work standards.

Wise management direction will avoid wasteful uses of this scarce talent. Before applying robotics and automation, studies should aim first at eliminating activities. Installing an automated storage warehouse to handle more efficiently inventory that is not really needed is folly. This is the kindest word I can think of to describe General Motors' plan in the early 1980s to regain the competitive lead in car production. After spending about $60 billion and 8 years redesigning all GM cars and automating all of its plants, its competitors—Ford, Chrysler, and Pacific Rim companies—still had lower costs. The best operation in GM was the New United Motors Manufacturing Plant in Fremont, California, in which they had invested very little in robotics and automation. They didn't understand and failed to apply elsewhere the lesson their Toyota partners in that plant taught them—*first simplify and eliminate, only then automate.*

In addition to these prerequisites for successful automation, there are ways in which most of the benefits of automation can be achieved for a small fraction of the costs. Hall's fine book, *Attaining Manufacturing Excellence*, (Bibl. 10), calls this, "Attaining the effect of automation without the expense." He describes many useful approaches to doing this.

Material Planning and Control

This group unites most closely the two flows of materials and information. Their basic responsibilities are to make sound, viable plans for necessary details of plant operations, compare actual performance (mainly of others) to plans, detect significant deviations from plan, and report them to those responsible for taking corrective actions. They must understand planning, execution, and control. The accepted definitions stated and discussed in Chapter 5 are

* Planning is the assignment of numbers to future events.
* Execution is the conversion of plans into reality.
* Control is the comparison of execution with plans, finding and highlighting significant deviations, and triggering corrective actions.

Sound execution and tight control recognize the fallibility of planning; no matter how well it is done or how powerful the systems used, there will always be some changes occurring during the planning horizon. Freezing a portion of the plan is counterproductive. It is equivalent to saying, "If we didn't plan it, we can't make it now" and also, "If we planned it, we must make it now whether we need it or not." Both are obvious fallacies and represent no way to run a fast, flexible, responsive manufacturing operation.

Planning must cover both capacity and priority requirements. Planners must understand and implement this principle:

19. Plan only capacity requirements over long horizons; schedule specific items only in the near future.

This recognizes that planning errors increase with the planning horizon. Capacity requirements planning, however, requires looking well ahead because of the relatively long times required to install new machines and equipment and train good workers. The errors of the longer horizon can be offset by the application of this principle:

20. Estimates of group totals for families of items will be more accurate than those of individual items.

Using family forecasts for groups of products provides better and fewer data for capacity planning. The actual times needed to make required batches of specific components and build individual products are a few hours, except for a very few products. If this is true, and it is, why should plans extend over weeks, months, and even years? Short-term schedules avoid committing resources to the wrong items. A common fallacy among both planning and production people is that starting work sooner will improve the chances of finishing on time. The next principle is difficult to sell:

21. Making anything too soon is a serious waste.

It is too easy to believe in the benefits of having more time to get work done and the need to avoid idle people and machines caused by material shortages. Not as well understood is the effect of releasing work too early. This causes larger capital investment in work-in-process, longer lead times and less valid plans, many higher overhead costs, and less flexibility to meet customers' needs promptly. It accomplishes exactly the opposite of what it is intended to do.

Planning must be constantly alert to avoid increasing work-in-process. This is done by matching actual work input to output in plant facilities. *The rule is that input should always be less than or equal to output, never larger.* Following this, the work-in-process and lead times will decline constantly or, at worst, remain constant. The principle states

22. Input higher than output must trigger instant alerts.

This is so fundamental and important that it should be well known to and understood by everyone who can influence directly or indirectly the amount of work released to a facility. This includes everyone in management and many in lower organization levels.

Quality Control

The 1960s, 1970s, and 1980s saw fundamental changes in the ways in which quality was controlled. Prior to this period, inspection was predominant; the good pieces were separated from the bad by indirect labor inspecting all pieces. When applicable, go/no-go gages, templates, and other mechanical aids were provided to eliminate human judgment; where people's sight, feeling, or hearing were necessary, the results were uncertain, at best. Significant amounts of rejects escaped notice and much good work was rejected.

The introduction and spread of statistical quality control techniques limited inspection to a small sample and focused attention on the production process as well as the product. It allowed a significant number of rejects (Acceptable quality level = 2%, for example). Experts with special training and skills were required to staff the QC department and, in many companies, they had the power to shut down operations if quality levels fell below standard. They reached their pinnacle in the 1970s when many companies tried "zero defects" programs, unfortunately with little success.

The 1980s brought a return to basic truths:

*   Products must be made right the first time.
*   The process must be controlled first.
*   The person who makes something is responsible for its quality.
*   Mistakeproof devices can help workers detect rejects.

* Rejects must be found immediately after they are made.
* Processes making rejects must be corrected immediately.
* Rejects must never be moved to the next operation.
* Statistical techniques can be learned by anyone and used to identify the problems causing rejects.

It is now generally accepted that *true quality control lies with those who operate the production processes.* Many, however, have not yet accepted the practicality of a goal of no rejects although companies in the United States as well as in Japan are regularly producing defect levels below two parts per million. The roles of staff experts are to educate and assist those who produce, not to catch their errors, second guess and overrule them.

Production

As noted in Chapter 2, from a position of preeminence immediately after World War II as leaders of "the arsenal of democracy," production managers have been demoted to the rank of second-class citizens in the industrial management hierarchy. This must be corrected. Their role should be equal, not inferior, to that of marketing, engineering, and financial people. To earn this, they must become more professional in their own areas, develop broader understanding of the other functions and their interrelationships, and prove that they can make an important contribution to strategic planning and improving their company's competitive position.

Contrast an airline pilot's professional stature, reputation, and leadership role with that of a typical manufacturing plant manager. Don't forget to contrast also the training and educational requirements for both. This comparison is valid also for other top-level managers. It is a moot question, "Which have the higher potential to do more harm to the greater number of human beings, poor pilots or poor executives in industry?"

The most difficult change for line production people and their supervisors to make is to accept the fact that *problems they face every day can be solved.* It is traditional to speak wryly of Murphy's Law and unavoidable upsets and to view production problems as unsolvable. This is soothing but false: Many problems in production can be eliminated; all can be attacked successfully to minimize their effects on plant operations.

Conventional wisdom says that suppliers will be late, some purchased and manufactured components will be defective, and machines and tooling will break down and that these and many other problems are inevitable. The accepted solution is to provide cushions of time, inventory, and capacity to blunt their effects on operations. Well-run companies recognize that such solutions are snares and delusions and now view such problems as intolerable.

Other widely held concepts must be changed. These statements are true: "Inventory is evil; you are better off without it"; "Nothing will be allowed to delay the flow of information and materials"; "The best lead times are the shortest." Strong educational efforts will be needed to convince production people that their long-held beliefs in the opposites are wrong and that these statements are true.

Gaining and maintaining a strong competitive position requires increasing the flexibility of manufacturing operations to make them more responsive to market needs. The single most important message in this book is that flows of materials and information must be faster. I have referred to the "glacial" pace of materials moving through production operations.

Many executives are unaware that this is true in their plants. I asked one chief executive officer if he believed materials sat untouched at least 90% of the time they were on the plant floor. He didn't, so I suggested a way to measure it. A few weeks later I received a letter telling me the results. It said, "We studied 79 orders completed in a two-week period and found to our amazement that

* The average percentage of time parts were worked on was less than 4%.
* 26 orders (about one-third) were completed ahead of schedule *by an average of 139 days* (my italics) and tied up about $75,000 in excess component stocks.
* A second study of another 51 orders showed parts worked on only 3% of the time and 12 orders (24%) completed an average of 94 days early, tying up even more capital.

This simple study convinced the CEO that attention to reducing excess work-in-process and stockroom inventories would pay off handsomely. He found when it was done that critical shortages of components were also reduced and, with them, the costs generated by expediting. Ability to make better promises and to deliver to customers on time was also enhanced greatly.

Amazingly, Henry Ford's Dearborn, Michigan, plant in 1910 (Bibl. 6) converted iron ore to automobiles in about 83 hours and had only 3 days of inventory, thus achieving 80 inventory turns. In 1985, Ford, Chrysler, and General Motors got only 10 to 15 turns; Henry's lessons were forgotten. Toyota was the standout car maker with about 70 turns; they learned them well.

By early 1965, my associates and I at The Stanley Works had proved the value of cutting lead times in intermittent batch manufacturing of hand tools. The *Executive's Bulletin* (Bibl. 4) explained what we had done—physically removed excess backlogs from the plant floor, tracked jobs with a simple color-coded tag system to identify any sitting more than two days in any work center, broke them loose, and released only work the plant could start on immediately. When asked about the risk of idle workers, we said, "Of course, some downtime is inevitable...but...it's a small price to pay for what we've gained." Many managers disagreed with this statement; to them idle workers and low machine utilization caused by lack of materials were the most heinous crime. They had been ignoring the high price paid to avoid such downtime.

Shortly afterward, Art Steinbruck, the foreman of Stanley's Yankee push screwdriver and drill line, ran a just-in-time "pull system" operation—although he did not know that's what it would be called a decade later. He aimed *to replace daily the tools that had been shipped the day before.* Here's how he did it:

* Each morning he would get from the finished goods warehouse a list of Yankee tools shipped the day before.
* He checked work orders for open balances authorizing production of these tools, usually no problem.
* He checked stockroom inventories for components needed to build the tools. Some shortages were common.
* If his people made the parts, they worked on shortages that day and could usually make enough.
* Shortages of parts made in another department required a visit or telephone call to get them made, often that day, rarely more than two days later.

In effect, Art Steinbruck replaced immediately in finished goods inventory tools that customers had taken out. He had work orders issued by materials planning people to build big (economical) lots of tools to scheduled dates and to make the components required, as did other work centers run by other supervisors. The planning system used lead times in weeks to determine related schedules.

Art and other supervisors knew that their people and machines could make small lots of parts and tools in a few hours, if they had the materials. The principle here is

23. Planning defines the resources needed to make what is planned; execution applies the resources available to make what customers want now.

Planning is approximate, at best. Execution is exact. Very little that is manufactured takes more than a few hours; why does planning use weeks, months, and years for lead times?

Purchasing

Purchasing's role needs reevaluation and revision. Among the silly cliches familiar to everyone in manufacturing is purchasing's statement, "Nobody talks to our vendors but us." Most of their talking, however, is simply parroting messages, relaying information from someone (typically in engineering, quality control, or material control) who knows what is needed to someone (usually the suppliers' salesperson) who can arrange to supply it. Handling all communications with suppliers requires far too much of their time and efforts. Expediting, rescheduling, and relaying change orders take precedence over their primary job, exactly like that of marketing/sales, of gathering the best information available on their suppliers and their marketplace.

In very few companies are purchased materials and services less than 50% of the cost of goods sold; in some it exceeds 70%. Procurement people are involved in more of a company's expenditures than any other organization group. Their best contribution to their firm's competitive position would obviously be finding better suppliers of needed goods and services.

Conventional wisdom among purchasing people (and many other executives) holds that having a bevy of competing suppliers for each commodity will result in the lowest material costs, the best quality materials, and the most reliable deliveries. This "wisdom" persists in spite of overwhelming evidence in decades of experience that it is not true. This principle applies:

24. One ace partner beats a full house of competing suppliers.

Convincing purchasing people that there is a better way requires strong direction by top management, who must themselves be convinced. There is strong evidence now, however, in every type of industry, that the best approach is setting up long-term "partnership" relations with a few "certified" suppliers. All information on purchased materials and services and their use by the customer is shared openly with these, along with the substantial savings that accrue from these partnerships.

Purchasing's primary task is *finding and certifying suppliers and coordinating the work of smoothing out and speeding up the flows of information to them and materials from them.* Their strategic contribution to their company's operations is gathering intelligence in the marketplace to prevent "surprises" and interruptions in supply. Culture shock is a mild term to apply to the changes required in purchasing.

Maintenance and Plant Engineering

Reliability of tooling, fixtures, machines, test, and other equipment is paramount in maintaining competitive operations. Breakdown repairs are expensive. Inventories of spare parts and supplies require large amounts of capital. Here too great changes in the way of life of maintenance and plant engineering people are needed.

The focus must shift from repairing breakdowns after they occur to preventive maintenance. Data on mean time between failures must be accumulated and maintained to ensure replacing critical parts of mechanical equipment before they fail. This is particularly important for plant utilities; failure of these can shut down major sections of operations, expose employees to serious injuries and health hazards, and also cause pollution of the environment. Conversely, energy, water used in the process; and other utilities offer great opportunities for significant savings.

When unexpected failures do occur (and they will!) the organization must be geared for rapid response and corrective action. Maintenance stores and spare parts require much more professional management than they get in most companies. The process industries are the exception and provide the example others should follow.

THE CHANGING ROLES OF STAFF "EXPERTS"

American workers have been oversupervised and undermanaged. Their work time has been clocked; the operations sequenced and detailed; machines, tooling, and test equipment provided; and their "efficiency" measured to two decimal places. They have not been trusted with "confidential" and "proprietary" information, nor consulted about better methods except through tedious suggestion plans with picayune rewards.

This is changing fast. Workers are now perceived as the unique resource not available to competitors. Many tasks previously reserved for management are now being assigned to workers. Planning, setting performance goals and measures, and developing and introducing process and product changes are included. The ingenuity and individuality of the American worker leads that of contemporaries throughout the world; this is now being recognized and utilized by enlightened managers to enhance progress.

Among the most wrenching and difficult changes needed is the shift of special skills from staff experts to production workers. It is now widely accepted that high quality can be achieved only if work is done correctly at the source. This concept must be applied also to manufacturing engineering activities (tool design, cutting setup times, developing flowlines, for example) and to maintenance.

Industrial engineers, quality control specialists, and plant engineers should be viewed as a "utility," providing their special skills and abilities to those individuals actually performing the operations and carrying out the activities. Essentially, this will require a shift from "doing it for them" to "teaching them to do it," a vastly different role for all parties involved.

This shift has been accepted widely in the elimination of separate inspectors; operators are provided with needed test and gauging equipment to determine when their work is acceptable. Even more important, this makes possible early detection of the process going out of control, before defects are made. Now popular, the shift from product to process control has proliferated, extending backward into suppliers' operations to make possible the elimination of both defects and incoming inspection.

The experience of many companies has proven the effectiveness of teaching machine operators the techniques for shortening setup times. Dramatic reductions of up to 90% have been achieved in a few weeks with little capital investment. Using engineers, no matter how skilled, cannot accomplish this as fast and certainly would not receive as quick acceptance by workers.

While actual repairs cannot be shifted to machine operators, they can be taught to play a vital role in detecting early warning signals of problems. Having operators watch for oil leaks, listen for strange noises, feel unusual warmth or vibrations, and even smell abnormal odors requires little training and returns large rewards by avoiding production interruptions and reducing repair costs. Minimizing problems through proper care of their machines during operations adds benefits at very little cost.

One important lesson from the success of Japanese companies seems to be ignored or overlooked by many observers and writers. It is illustrated by the experiences of W. Edwards Deming, one of the recognized gurus of statistical quality control. He has been telling the same story since the 1930s. In the United States, his message was, and often still is, interpreted to require setting up quality control departments of "experts" who (1) monitored production, (2) shut the process down when defects exceeded permissible limits, and (3) helped identify the basic causes.

The Japanese heard it differently. They learned quickly how statistical methods provide assistance in identifying when a manufacturing process is out of control, even providing clues before it goes out. They exposed all production workers to the techniques, providing them with tools to enhance their abilities to catch and solve problems quickly *before rejects were made*. In addition, they taught the same techniques to supervisors, managers, and executives so that all were aware of the superior power of process control over inspection sorting good product from bad.

The proper role of the experts is to teach their special skills and techniques to those who do the work. Cadres of staff experts on the periphery of operations can never be as effective as fully qualified workers doing the processing.

Specialization of labor must be replaced by broad-based training in the many techniques people need to do their work, do it properly, and do it with as little direct assistance as possible from staff experts. Quality control, process, plant layout and test engineers, schedulers, material handlers, and many others normally classified as "overhead" or "indirect" can be more effective and fewer in number if they become teachers, not doers.

CHAPTER 7

Measures
of Performance

It is easy to be swamped with data while starving from lack of information.

SUMMARY

Financial accounting systems have served well the needs of top-level executives and outsiders interested in companies' performances but have not been as useful to managers making internal operating decisions. Manufacturing has changed dramatically and new measures are needed to evaluate modern manufacturing practices. Measures must relate to three objectives—satisfying customers, cutting costs, and using capital better. When the wrong measures are used, poor decisions result. Direct labor efficiency, direct material costs, book value of machinery, and return on investment are examples.

Modern data processing equipment has tempted people to collect too much data; good communications requires filtering real signals from static. Precision is not accuracy, and timeliness must take precedence over completeness. Aggregates are better than details, physical measures better than financial, and visual feedback more useful than systems data. The hierarchy of performance measures includes external activities, the total business, plant-level performance, and work center activities.

Effective performance measurement requires suppressing masses of trivial data and focusing on vital facts. Conventional measures do not include the really important ones, and new financial and physical measures must be applied. In addition, each department has applicable specific measures common to most businesses.

The essence of control is valid planning, prompt execution, timely, accurate feedback, and fast solutions to problems. Challenging goals stimulate eliminating activities or doing different things, not just doing the same things better. The right performance measures communicate desired objectives to all and also focus managements' attention on the important problems. Cost accounting and management reporting systems have been designed for the scorekeepers; the players' needs must also be met.

THE NEED TO CHALLENGE TRADITION

Financial data produced by conventional cost accounting and management reporting systems have been effective and will continue to be used to provide information about a company's performance to executives and outsiders. The stockholders, investment community, government agencies, and the public as well as executives in the corporate family need such data in familiar, standardized formats.

Unfortunately, financial data in conventional charts of accounts, on budgets, and for traditional measures of performance have not and will not meet the needs of those directly responsible for improving the performance of manufacturing companies. Looked at objectively, such systems appear to be designed for the scorekeepers, not the players in the manufacturing game. Radical changes are needed.

Traditional accounting and reporting systems have provided managers with masses of data; much of it is worthless in making operating decisions. Those now in companies successfully implementing modern manufacturing strategies like flexible machining systems (FMS), just-in-time (JIT), and continuous flow manufacturing (CFM) see most clearly the need for different and more pertinent performance measures. Even though not so evident, they are needed in all manufacturing firms.

Manufacturing operations have changed rapidly and dramatically recently, but accounting practices and performance reporting have not kept pace. The responsibility for this lies primarily on operations managers, not accountants, because they accepted the situation. In fact, many have not yet recognized that their needs have changed. Making the needed revisions will require the combined efforts of accountants and operations managers; the latter must lead the way.

Conventional accounting and financial reporting systems have failed to aid manufacturing management in making many decisions affecting competitive position. The three most important factors in a company's competitive strength are

* Ability to satisfy, not just serve, its customers.
* Unrelenting attacks on all costs to produce adequate profit margins on all products.
* Constant reductions in capital requirements.

Even a quick analysis will show clearly how little help such systems give decision makers in these three areas. Many items in a typical chart of accounts, although easy to get, are trivial; important factors difficult to quantify are ignored.

Charts of accounts accumulate data in arbitrary categories little related to tough, important decisions operations managers must make. Here are some examples:

Satisfying Customers

Selling prices are easy to quantify and compare to those of competitors. Much more difficult, and yet very important to customers, are speed of response to changes, flexibility in applying resources to meet current actual demand, and the times required for delivery. Figure 7–1 shows some potential benefits to delight customers and suppliers alike as operations are improved. These data are compiled from the actual experiences of my clients over many years.

Figure 7–1 Customer Service Benefits

On-Time Deliveries	Up 85 - 98%
Delivery Times	Down 25 - 75%
New Product Introduction Time	Down 20 - 50%
Salespeople's Productivity	Up 20 - 40%
Internal Sales Costs	Down 50 - 90%
Excess Freight Costs	Down 75 - 90%

A budget for research and development expenditures is a precise number, but undefined and missing are the factors which cause it to take so long to introduce new products and how much it would cost to shorten that time. This will become much more important in satisfying customers and, at the same time, more difficult as the rate of change continues to accelerate. In spite of its being our scarcest and most valuable resource, time data are missing and their value is neither represented nor recognized in conventional accounting systems.

To decide whether to continue making individual products or to discontinue them, the correct profit margins on individual products are vital information. Rules used commonly to allocate overhead costs make it easy to get the wrong answers. Relating overhead to direct labor content penalizes mature, high-volume items and understates costs of new, difficult-to-make ones. This topic is covered in greater detail in the section Financial Measures of Performance later in this chapter.

Reducing Costs

Budgets and performance data contain myriad costs which are trivial but typically show variances on all items. Exception reports highlighting the few important variances are rare. Continuing use of such data over several years develops the knee-jerk reaction of spending some time on each variance analyzing causes and developing corrections. The targeted percentage reduction in each cost is accepted as good performance. This is not only a rank waste of valuable management time and energy; such mind-sets also result in *failure to recognize the possibility of eliminating many costs, not just reducing them.*

Figure 7–2 shows the changes over three decades in factory costs, together with a prognosis for the future. As a percentage of total factory costs, direct labor (DL) costs have decreased dramatically. Blue-collar labor's share of total cost is now too small to be a significant competitive factor in most companies; this change has resulted from simplifying product designs and increasing labor productivity.

Material (MAT'L) costs have remained about the same and overhead costs have grown significantly. Variable overhead (VOH), changing with production volume, has dropped, but fixed overhead (FOH) costs associated with buildings, machines, and other capital assets have grown and will continue to be a higher proportion of factory costs in the future. As

Figure 7–2 Factory Cost Changes

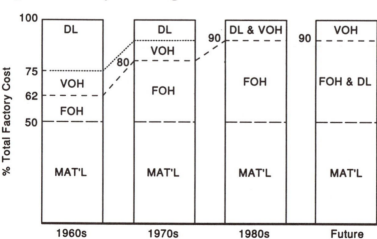

direct labor takes on its full role, including not only production but also quality control, scheduling, operations improvement, and maintenance duties, the costs associated with these highly skilled people will be viewed as fixed, not variable.

Detailed cost data are available in conventional costing systems on many activities usually considered overhead—incoming and process inspection, material handling, storerooms, and many clerical tasks. Strong efforts are made, usually periodically, to reduce these costs. These are misdirected; the best approach is to work to eliminate such redundant activities entirely. Some specific ways to do this are described in Chapter 6.

Mathematical techniques based on intellectually elegant theories— economic order quantities, statistical safety stocks, and optimized scheduling are examples—focus attention on a few costs needed for the calculations. Other costs relevant to the decisions are ignored and may be more important than those used.

Improvements in the flows of materials and information have been cited throughout this book as basic requirements for better performance. Faster, smoother, and more continuous movement, and better balanced operations produce many significant benefits. If components of products are made in matched sets in small lots at frequent intervals and products are completed steadily, the effects on costs can be substantial. Reductions will appear in

* Inventory investment and carrying costs—few materials are needed to cope with erratic, unbalanced needs, and fewer surpluses are generated in production.
* Material costs—less wastage and scrap.
* Labor costs—steady production is always more efficient.
* Tooling costs—more common tools for families of parts.
* Obsolescence losses—less material is in process and in inventory to be affected by engineering or customer delivery changes.
* Planning and control costs—systems are simpler.
* Guarantee and field service costs—higher-quality and improved design products perform better.

Coupled with these cost reductions, many other substantial improvements are realized in operations and related activities:

* On-time deliveries—customer service levels of 95% and higher are common.
* Flexibility—faster response to changes in customer requirements.
* New product introduction—shorter time to design, develop, test, and produce new models and product lines.

Reductions in Capital Requirements

Most companies make some serious attempt to determine how much capital costs when it is invested in inventory and machinery. Very few really know how much inventory is needed in running the business and the right level of machine utilization. Compared to total machine costs per hour, which are easily calculated, what is the value of unused capacity which would permit quick deliveries on unexpected "windfall" orders? When added capacity is needed, which alternative is preferable: invest in additional machines, hire more people, work overtime, or send work to outside firms? Managers making such choices get little if any help from today's systems since data on many relevant factors are not in cost systems.

Financial and accounting systems often are updated by transactions different from those used in operations. For example, material added to inventory in financial accounts is reported by means of suppliers' invoices. Physical records are increased by receiving reports, modified by incoming inspection. The multitude of transactions, timing differences, and error-prone handling of data result in significant differences between financial and physical records. Such errors are costly and reconciliation of these differences wastes much valuable time and distorts profits.

DECISION MAKING WITH THE WRONG NUMBERS

Conventional wisdom among many financial executives and in the business schools states that any professional manager can run any company because he "knows how to read the numbers." Implicit in this statement is the belief that a sound knowledge of how individual manufacturing firms can and should be operated is not required. This misconception has been a major factor in the decline of American industry in the recent past. *The numbers are not the business; they show only one picture of it.*

Also implicit in the statement is an assumption that the right numbers will be recognized and available. Here are a few examples of how reading the wrong numbers, or failing to get the right ones, leads to bad decisions:

Direct Labor Efficiency

Direct labor costs have had very close scrutiny since Frederick W. Taylor and his peers introduced scientific management in the last decade of the nineteenth century. Skilled industrial engineers have worked diligently in the interim to develop efficient workstation layouts and to set time standards on operations performed in them. Used to measure and control direct labor, this effort produced very significant improvements in performance. U.S. productivity was higher than that of every country in the world through the 1970s, but this is no longer true.

Direct labor efficiency measures are counterproductive in improving real productivity in several ways:

1. **They lull managers to sleep.** Workers will usually achieve acceptable efficiencies in work on standard. This leads ingenuous managers to believe that performance is satisfactory. Direct labor efficiency is a precise ratio of standard time allowed to actual time taken for specific operations measured. Direct labor productivity is very different. It is the actual total labor cost of producing the total output achieved. High labor efficiencies do not indicate high productivity when workers spend significant time on nonstandard work, however permissible it may be. Reducing or eliminating such nonstandard work is far more productive than improving labor efficiency and much easier. Also, when indirect labor is needed to help direct workers achieve high efficiencies, total productivity may be low even while direct labor efficiency is high.

2. **They are too costly and impractical.** Even small firms must maintain massive data files and employ powerful data collection and processing equipment to compute labor efficiencies. In the past, few companies had even 90% complete coverage with engineered standards and many were obsolete; it will be impossible to get near this level and to keep standards current with the accelerating rate of changes in methods, tooling, and machinery needed in the future if companies are to be more competitive.

3. **They engender antagonism.** Long ago it was learned that experienced workers who perform production operations usually know better methods than those prescribed by the standards. In the past, they suppressed such knowledge, using it sub rosa for their own advantage. Stimulating workers' desire to cooperate with each other and with management is the open secret of continuing gains in productivity. Setting, applying, and revising standards have been frequent causes of friction between labor unions and management; removing these is worthwhile.

4. **They waste scarce resources.** All the cream and most of the milk were skimmed off by these methods by the early 1970s. Productivity improvements, automation, and robotics have shrunk direct labor costs further; only a small fraction of manufacturing companies now have direct labor costs above 10% of total factory cost; many are less than 5%. Most, however, still employ highly skilled engineers to set time standards. This wastes the efforts of a very scarce resource—manufacturing engineers, who ought to be working on smoothing out and speeding up the flow of materials to achieve far greater improvements in performance.

5. **They misdirect robotics and automation.** In this country, applications of such equipment have been focused on high-volume products of stable designs to reduce direct labor. These applications are characterized by lack of flexibility to react to changes in products or processes as market needs vary and new technologies are introduced. The $60 billion debacle in General Motors' 1979-1986 plan to automate its plants, discussed in Chapter 6, is tragic evidence of this misperception.

The focus on high direct labor cost operations as candidates for automation also ignores opportunities for significant benefits in reduced costs of low-volume products. Setting the proper goals for automation and robotics—*increasing flexibility and reducing direct and indirect labor and material costs*—results in many more and much better applications implemented in less time at much lower cost.

Concentration on direct labor efficiency often causes serious side effects. Here's a typical scenario

* A worker performing secondary operations (not the starting ones) needs more work.
* Shop orders containing suitable work are issued earlier than needed.
* These orders are expedited through preceding centers to get them quickly to the threatened worker.

The worker is kept busy—but at the high costs of

* The expediting effort.
* The extra planning work to find and release orders.
* Higher investment in work-in-process.
* More shortages of urgent items needing the same raw materials or purchased components.
* Higher inventories of unneeded components.
* Higher rework or obsolescence costs of items started early and affected by engineering design or process changes.

Direct Material Costs

It is possible to get precise (although not necessarily accurate) values for the costs of materials used in manufactured products. Purchased material costs can be obtained from suppliers' invoices and value added in processing determined from direct labor and appropriate factory overhead costs. Direct comparisons with substitute materials available from foreign low-labor-cost suppliers often show that substantial savings are possible from buying instead of making these items. This is one of the principal causes of the large unfavorable U.S. trade balances of the 1980s.

In making such comparisons, however, several important factors which do not appear in conventional cost data are usually overlooked. These are

* Additional costs of ordering, follow-up, receiving, customs clearance, currency conversion, and delays.
* Cost of carrying large inventories in transportation pipelines.
* Problems of poor communications over long distances, in different time zones, and in foreign languages.
* Costs from problems remaining unresolved for longer periods.
* Costs related to slower reaction to needed changes.
* Effects of poorer customer service.

Potentially even more important than any or all of these is *transfer of manufacturing technology which inevitably accompanies purchase of materials,* particularly those requiring sophisticated processes, like machine tool and aircraft components, electronic appliances, semiconductors, and computers. In effect, companies buying such materials are giving away key elements of their businesses, setting up potential competitors. How else did the Japanese, Taiwanese, and Koreans get so good so fast in so many high-tech businesses? Recognizing this, many U.S. firms are bringing work back from foreign suppliers and not sending more.

Book Value of Machinery

These costs, like so many in conventional accounting systems, can be calculated easily—simply deduct accumulated depreciation from the original cost. The rules for handling depreciation allowances are set by people in government, usually lawyers, who have little understanding of the ways machinery loses either its useful or economic life. Their interest is primarily in the amount of revenue raised; the effects on industry of the rules are secondary. Too many managers who use these book values also lack full understanding of the numbers and their implications.

Book value is useless in making replacement decisions. Machines may be worn out physically, unable to produce materials to specifications, long before they are fully depreciated. If the firm is to be competitive, they must be replaced with similar or more modern, better machines. Conversely, machines may be in excellent physical condition and have a high book value but be economically worthless because better equipment is available to produce materials at much lower cost. The book value is again useless in replacement decisions. Too much emphasis on the residual book value of existing plant and the effects on current profits of writing this off resulted in failure of the U.S. steel industry to invest in new steel mills employing the latest technology when their competitors were doing just that.

Fully depreciated machines in good running condition can be used in productive ways by knowledgeable managers. A motorcycle plant has several good, small arbor presses fully depreciated; they also have modern tube-forming machines which are much more efficient. The presses are installed adjacent to the assembly line, each permanently set up with the dies to form a specific unique component used in small quantities on some varieties of motorcycles. The few high-volume parts are formed on the efficient machines; the permanent setups on the presses make possible forming odd parts, as motorcycles using them are being assembled on the line, with no setup cost and no formed-tube inventory. A savvy person knew the value of flexibility and fast response to needs; decisions were not based solely on book values and tube-forming costs.

Return on Investment

The spate of mergers, takeovers, and acquisitions—friendly and hostile—has been based mainly on analyses of many numbers. The principal ones used, of course, are the recent record of a company's earnings and stock price. Low price/earnings ratios identify the best candidates for takeover even though little, if anything, is known by the buyers about the firm's plans for the future or its ability to execute these plans well. Steering the ship by watching the wake is a good description of this approach. The implicit assumption that the company will continue to earn the same returns in the future (or even better returns to pay off the large debts of the takeover) is often fallacious.

On the other hand, a company performing poorly with low return on investment is apparently a good candidate for being sold off. Again, there is an implicit assumption that it cannot do better. Very few of those making such decisions have the understanding of manufacturing to evaluate this. Financiers, bankers, lawyers, and other outsiders engaged in this game of buying and selling companies rarely take the time and probably do not know how to evaluate the true potential of a company to perform better in the future; they must use the data they have and make fast decisions.

There is no excuse, however, for corporate executives to make important decisions on spinoffs and acquisitions on the bases of similar information and superficial analyses. They should know how their companies are being, and can and should be run. Good performance of manufacturing companies is too important to themselves, parent corporations, workers, stockholders, suppliers, and this nation's economy to risk errors from misreading numbers and from snap judgments. Additional discussion of return on investment is included in the section Financial Measures of Performance later in this chapter.

REQUIREMENTS FOR EFFECTIVE MEASUREMENT

The advent of computers, data collection terminals, and bar coding equipment has generated irresistible temptations in manufacturing to amass data on plant activities. Appearing to be so inexpensive, fast, and useful, sophisticated systems are developed to massage the data. Appearances are very deceptive. While the actual data handling may be cheap, the related costs of developing and implementing the system, analyzing the data, and acting on it build up high overhead costs. Much of the data collected en masse by such systems are like "noise" in radio transmission—loud but meaningless. Getting good communications and tight control require filtering the true signals from the static.

Pareto's principle applies to this as well as to many other sets of data; there are a few vital and many trivial pieces. The basic logic of manufacturing, stated in Chapter 1, must be understood before it is possible to identify the vital ones.

This principle governs all manufacturing data:

25. "Data" are simply facts; "information" requires facts having useful meanings.

For example, the location and status of every manufacturing order in a plant are data; the total number of orders open, whether or not this total is shrinking or growing in any work center and how many orders are really late are pieces of useful information. Such useful information can be extracted from data on the status of all orders; it can be determined much more simply and effectively from more direct performance measures. *The focus of data collection and performance measures must be on the vital few.* No data should be collected simply because it is easy or cheap to do so. Like marriage, the initial cost may be low but the ongoing expenses are not.

Traditional cost accounting and financial systems produce output reports for specific periods of time—last week, last month, the first quarter, for example—only after all data for the period have been accumulated and cross-checked. This process takes a significant amount of time. For control of operations, this principle applies:

26. Ninety-five percent complete information now is far better for control than 100% later.

As covered in Chapter 6, the essence of good control is timeliness. Deviations from plans requiring corrective actions must be detected as soon after they occur as possible and the necessary action determined and taken as quickly as practicable. Uncorrected problems continue to cause trouble, increasing in severity as time goes on. The watchwords are, "Find them and fix them fast." Waiting for complete data can be a handicap.

Incomplete information is often adequate to detect many serious problems—scrap, rework, late orders, interruptions are a few. Delays for system processing, clearing the paper pipeline, tracking lost transactions, and converting units of measure are intolerable. Visual and physical data are superior to financial data for the same reasons, covered in the next section of this chapter under the heading Physical Versus Financial Data.

Another principle of performance measurement is

27. The best measures of performance are aggregates, not details.

In this vein, the following general statements are true:

* Data on families of similar products, components, work centers, processes, and the like yield more useful information than those on specific items.
* Flow rates through work areas are better than quantities and dates on individual orders.
* Trends are more meaningful than absolute values. Rate of change shows more than a number at a point in time.
* Total manufacturing cycle times are more important than individual item lead times.
* Productivity of the whole company is much more important than efficiency of direct labor.
* Approximate values of the right measures are far more useful than exact figures of the wrong ones.

Aggregate numbers, almost invariably, are easier to get and to use than myriad details. Often, as is true of overall company productivity, they can be determined directly without adding up the constituent individual details.

Reporting actual performance data or showing planned or budgeted figures separately tells only half the story. This principle is a requirement for sound planning and control:

28. Any valid control report must show both planned and actual performance data.

During their development and to show future activities, plans can be reported separately. For historical records, actual performance can also be shown alone. For control purposes, however, *planned and actual data for recent and current periods must be shown side by side and significant deviations highlighted* to bring them to people's attention.

PHYSICAL VERSUS FINANCIAL DATA

While financial data are needed by and useful to many people in and outside a company, internally the use of physical data is necessary for effective control. H. Thomas Johnson (Bibl. 12) calls these types of data "activity based" and discusses many different examples in his excellent article. They have many distinct advantages. This principle is now recognized:

29. Physical units of measure are superior to financial.

Physical data are better for several important reasons:

* They are more timely, providing signals that something is amiss immediately as it happens.
* They are more specific and relevant, clearly identified with a cause at a location, not lumped with other similar occurrences in arbitrary groupings.
* They are simpler, easier, and cheaper to get on the spot and to see immediately.
* Errors from converting units of measure are avoided.
* Causes are more easily differentiated from symptoms and proper corrective actions determined.
* Accountability is clearer and more direct.

Another principle relevant to the best type of performance measures to use is

30. Visual feedback is preferable to system data.

Individuals alert to potential problems can initiate the most immediate, effective corrective actions when they witness some aberrations from norms. Visual feedback has all of the advantages over data produced by planning and control systems cited above for physical measures over financial. They are the purest sort of activity-based data.

THE HIERARCHY OF PERFORMANCE MEASUREMENT

The very presence of specific numbers in a control process compels people to think of and raise questions about the causes and effects related to the numbers. Every manager is familiar with the phenomenon of requesting and getting a new report and finding that it raises more questions than it answers. Charts of accounts, budgets, and other management reports have proliferated since the introduction of electronic data collection and processing equipment and managers see far more data than they can do anything about.

The popular technique called Management By Objectives is often applied to focus the organization's attention on part of the data to achieve some goal like reducing inventory, improving customer service, or increasing profit margins. These three have been edicts issued frequently and consecutively by executives.

I discussed this INSANE cycle (IN for "inventory," S for "service," ANE for "and net earnings") in *Manufacturing Control: The Last Frontier for Profits* (Bibl. 15) to show the impossibility of achieving these goals independently. I pointed out also that the effort generated more problems than it solved. Improvements in performance are possible only if the right measures are used and come quickly when the proper priority and resources are applied to actions required to meet them.

Measures of the performance of manufacturing companies are needed covering all phases of the business. These can be viewed as this hierarchy, with some details as indicated:

External Activities

Exceeding market demands for quality, price, delivery dependability, flexibility, and speed of response

Complying with government regulations on safety, health, and other matters

Protecting the environment

Generating earnings adequate to satisfy owners, potential investors, and lenders

Total Business Activities

Share of market

Growth rates of present products

Speed of introduction and growth rates of new products

Return on sales and capital employed

Cash flow

Debt/equity ratio

Plant Activities

Overall quality

Total direct materials, labor, and overhead costs

Production cycle times

Asset utilization

Gross profit

Work area activities

Quality of specific items produced

Direct materials and labor costs of specific items

Operation lead times
Productivity improvements
Individual machine and personnel performance
Schedule adherence

This book will not treat external and business activities; there is more than adequate coverage of these in the literature and no need exists to make significant changes in these measures of performance. Both are familiar areas to executives. The great and compelling need today is for a clearer understanding of the internal workings of manufacturing operations, long neglected in literature directed at top management.

New, improved methods of planning, execution, and control of manufacturing demand new performance measures. This chapter will focus attention on the important few relating to internal activities which have been missing, misapplied, or misunderstood by both managers and executives. This subject is treated also in my article, "Cost Accounting in Manufacturing: Dawn of a New Era" (Bibl. 21).

FINANCIAL MEASURES OF PERFORMANCE

Inventory Turnover Rates

The best single indicator of the effectiveness of management of a manufacturing company is the rate at which inventory turns. This is calculated from

$$\text{Turnover Rate} = \text{Shipments} / \text{Inventory}$$

Turns can be measured using inventory priced at actual or standard cost, shipments at cost or selling price, average inventory over a period, or total inventory at the beginning or end of the period. As long as they are used consistently, it makes little difference which numbers are used. Because of these differences, however, comparisons of turnover rates for different companies are of questionable meaning.

Further evidence of lack of control of manufacturing is the behavior of inventory. After every recession, management resolves that they will get tighter control and prevent future large excesses like those just experienced. The next downturn, however, finds them wondering what caused the large excesses this time but just as strongly resolved to avoid it again.

Contrary to popular belief, inventory is not an independent variable subject to individual control. It is rather the result of the interactions of many activities, problems, and failings. Every organizational group can (and probably does) contribute to a company's inventory. One of the major contributing groups is top management; every error in decisions that they make shows up as excess inventory sooner or later. Only brief thought is required to see the truth of this statement.

Other groups are culprits also. Design engineering through poor designs and frequent engineering changes, process engineering through unbalanced flow rates and long machine setups, plant engineering through poor maintenance and plant layout, marketing and sales through poor intelligence of customers' real needs, labor unions through restrictive work rules, production workers through poor quality, and everyone through record errors (and the compelling need to have cushions) contribute to inventory.

Practically all executives and managers watch turnover rates and issue edicts or make plans for improving them. Unfortunately, their aspirations are usually much too modest. Most American manufacturing companies have turnover rates between 2 and 6 and would like about 25–30% improvement (e.g., from 2 to 3, 4 to 5). Such modest expectations will cause people to work harder but will not force them to work smarter. They will never generate the innovative actions which will increase turnover dramatically. *It is neither impossible nor unrealistic in most companies to aim to double the present turnover* (cut existing inventories in half) in the next 12 months. Turnover rates in double digits are possible in most manufacturing companies.

With improved operations, Figure 7–3 shows potential reductions in several categories of inventory. It is based on my experience in many companies in different industries. These are conservative figures. Note that the two classes of repair parts and the tooling group are materials which do not go into products but they also represent significant capital investments.

Figure 7–3 Potential Inventory Reductions

Raw Materials	20 - 40%
Purchased and Manufactured Parts	20 - 40%
Safety Stock	50 - 95%
Work-in-Process	25 - 75%
Finished Products	10 - 40%
Tooling, Gages, Fixtures, etc.	20 - 40%
Repair Parts (Customers' Use)	25 - 50%
Repair Parts (Factory's Use)	40 - 60%
Obsolete Materials	50 - 90%

Here are a few examples of the reductions in total inventory made by aggressive management in three years or less:

Twist drills, 92%	Chain saw bars, 29%
Gun cleaning kits, 94%	Gun reloading kits, 50%
Valve handles, 98%	Outboard motors, 50%
Steel buildings, 75%	Copying machines, 30%

Before any executives conclude that comparable cuts cannot be made in their companies, they should walk through their plants looking at the masses of materials lying idle on the work floors, in stockrooms, and in receiving, inspection, and similar areas.

Return on Capital Employed

Return on investment is a very common measure of a company's overall performance. It takes many forms, however, some more meaningful to competitive performance than others. Several versions of both terms, investment and return, are used. Return, or profits, can be gross, operating, before taxes, or after taxes. Since taxes are a significant part of costs, particularly in the United States, profit after taxes is much more meaningful in measuring competitive ability.

Capital invested is expressed in many ways also. Stockholders' equity, a popular one, is the difference between assets and liabilities, not just a measure of capital. This tempts many executives to play financial games, like buying back company stock, to make things look better. If this uses capital which is needed to improve operations, it is counterproductive.

Other ways to express capital invested vary more from types of funding than from operating characteristics. The most indicative of sound performance is capital employed, which measures the money invested in the business. Hence, *return (total profits after taxes) on investment (total capital used in operations)* is the most useful ratio when measuring overall performance.

In the United States, there is intense competition for available capital. This includes the enormous federal deficit, a crippling unfavorable balance of trade, and many nonmanufacturing uses. Coupled with low U.S. savings rates, inadequate generation of new wealth from declining manufacturing, stumbling agriculture, and sick extraction industries provides smaller amounts of capital. The two effects combine to place a premium on more productive uses of capital in manufacturing.

Aggregate Production-Sales-Inventory

A very useful report is shown in Figure 7–4, combining aggregate totals for the three major interdependent variables, shipments, production and inventory, of interest to management. This is often called an inventory input/output report since it shows totals of input and output and their influence on total inventory. It uses the equation expressing the relations among the three variables:

Beginning Inventory + Production - Shipments = Ending Inventory

The report can be set up for whole companies, individual plants, product families, or specific work areas. Time periods are weekly or monthly. In Figure 7–4, covering one product family made in a single plant, production has been subdivided into purchased material and productive labor inputs. Better results are obtained when shipments (or sales) data are costs, unaffected by special discounts, promotions, and other selling price changes.

The plan for this product family is to cut total inventories by 20% in the next year. Based on sales forecasts, total shipments are spread throughout the year with a significant increase in March (seasonal products?). The purchased material input rate can be calculated most simply by determining the purchase content of the cost of goods sold and prorating the reduction for the year over the individual months. A similar calculation for labor will give its input plan. More refined data are not needed.

When computer-based planning and control systems are in use, much more detailed calculations of material and labor requirements can be made based on released and planned purchase and manufacturing orders and specific product shipments. It is questionable, however, that such precision will substantially improve the accuracy of the simple estimates. Actual performance data are easily found in most companies' systems.

Figure 7–4 Inventory Input/Output Report

Inventory Jan. 1   = $3,000,000
Goal   Dec. 31 = $3,000,000

Month	Purchase Material Plan	Act.	Dev.	Production Labor Plan	Act.	Dev.	Shipments Plan	Act.	Dev.	Inventory Plan	Act.	Dev.
Jan.	240	260	20	160	150	(10)	450	430	(20)	2,950	2,980	30
Feb.	240	230	(10)	160	165	5	450	470	20	2,900	2,905	5
Mar.	270	260	(10)	180	175	(5)	500	480	(20)	2,850	2,860	10
Apr.	270			180			500			2,800		
Etc.												

In January, Figure 7–4 shows labor and shipments both below plan (cause and effect?), purchases well above plan, and inventory above budget as a result. Seeing this at the end of the month, individuals responsible for allocation of labor to this product family took corrective actions to get the required people, those supervising production pressed for increased shipments, and materials planning and purchasing people screened orders arriving during February to get back on plan. The actual data for February show how successful they all were.

This example was taken from a make-to-stock company. One with custom-built products would be concerned with total booked orders, not finished goods inventory. An identical type of report can be produced showing input of newly booked orders, output of shipments, and total booked orders in lieu of inventory. In a make-to-order business, production (purchased materials and productive labor) for each period can be assumed to be equal to shipments. Here the arithmetic is

Beginning Bookings + New Orders - Shipments (= Production) = Ending Bookings

The sources of data are self-evident and the use of the report is the same as for Figure 7– 4—to alert people early to the need for corrective actions, using a few aggregate measures.

Product Profit Margins

As was mentioned earlier in this chapter in the section The Need to Challenge Tradition, the allocation of overhead costs to materials and products based on direct labor content is no longer valid. In the past, direct material and labor comprised the bulk of the cost of manufactured products and varied directly with output rates. Overhead activities were largely related to supporting labor and also varied with labor costs. Even capital resources were used to enhance direct labor and tended to be constant over long time periods since product designs and process technologies changed slowly. All of these relationships have now changed dramatically.

Design and technology changes come at an accelerating rate. Labor costs have dropped significantly as a percentage of factory cost while fixed overhead expenses have risen sharply and now constitute the bulk of such costs (see Figure 7–2). For these reasons, allocating overhead to products based on direct labor content is not only inaccurate but misleading.

A recognized phenomenon is shown in Figure 7–5. The vertical scale is percent of total sales and total overhead costs. Following Pareto's law, a very few (so-called A) products bring in the bulk of sales income but incur little overhead cost. The largest share of overhead

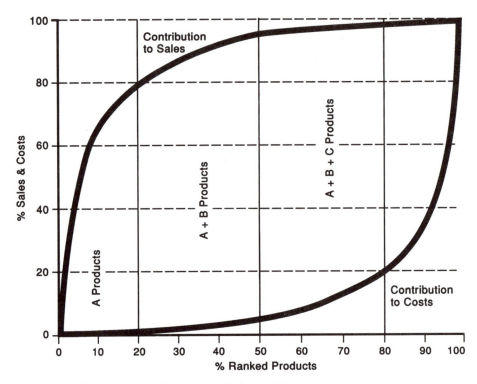

Figure 7–5 Product Contributions to Sales and Cost

costs are related to the many (C) products generating a small portion of income. Rational ways are needed to charge products with their proper share of overhead.

Categories of overhead expenses in conventional charts of accounts must be restructured to identify cost with cause. Here are a few examples: receiving department activities are related to the number of purchased components they handle and the number of different suppliers used; incoming inspection costs are a function of the number of components, suppliers, and difficulties in meeting specifications; expenses of a materials control department, including computer-based systems used, are determined by the sophistication of such systems, the frequency of changes in plans and the difficulties experienced executing plans.

All significant causes of overhead costs must be identified with specific products so that these bear their proper share. To many managers this seems extremely difficult but only because they have not tried to do it. Conventional cost systems use categories of things easy to count; these must be changed to those that really count in determining accurate profit margins. The decisions based on such margins affecting selling prices, profit, market opportunities, and utilization of scarce resources are too important to delay getting this tough job started. Too few firms have seen this clearly and are working on it.

Productivity

Volumes have been written on techniques for calculating productivity of direct labor, most using efficiency based on time standards. Little has been published on ways to determine productivity of non-direct people, including indirect and those whom Peter Drucker calls knowledge workers. Efforts to improve the former have been wonderfully successful and continue to show steady gains. As illustrated by the poor performance of service industries—banking, insurance, the professions—the expensive computers expected to improve productivity of people in such firms have yet to begin to pay off the enormous investment.

Using financial data, determining the overall productivity of all individuals in a firm is a very simple calculation:

Productivity = Output at Cost / Wages and Salaries

In addition to being simpler, this is much more meaningful than the direct labor efficiencies used by most companies. Its calculation was shown in the earlier section of this chapter titled, Decision Making with the Wrong Numbers, along with comments on other problems caused by using direct labor time standards and efficiencies.

Many of my clients have had direct labor efficiencies of 125–150% and higher, earned by working "efficiently" a small part of the time; such measures give misleading impressions of productivity. Poor direct labor performance doing unmeasured work and low output of indirect labor, staff, and clerical people can easily eat up all the high efficiency gains.

Strong competition will force companies *to enlist all people in improving the ways everything is done or, even better, eliminating the need to do many things*. These bring real productivity gains. The accelerating rate of change in products, processes, and people's skills will make it prohibitively expensive to get and maintain work standards. Other simpler, less expensive ways must be found to set standards without tying up valuable engineers needed to smooth out and speed up the flow of materials.

Here are a few examples of productivity gains in successful companies:

Hammers, 29%	Twist drills, 30%
P.C. Boards, 50%	Chain saw bars, 30%
Steel buildings, 39%	Copying machines, 23%

Note that these figures are from eight to ten or more times the average U.S. productivity gains in the last three decades. More on productivity measured in nonfinancial terms appears in the following section of this chapter.

PHYSICAL MEASURES OF PERFORMANCE

The advantages of physical measures of performance over financial and systems-generated data were presented earlier in this chapter under the heading, Requirements for Effective Measurement. Some important physical performance measures are the following:

Time Periods of Supply

This is analogous to inventory turnover but often is much easier to measure in physical units. The arithmetic of the calculation is

Quantity on Hand / Quantity Used per Period = Time Periods of Supply

This ratio can be determined easily for any class of inventory—raw materials, work-in-process, finished products, supplies, and any others—in any or all locations throughout a manufacturing plant or a distribution system. The quantity on hand is taken directly from inventory balance records. The rate of use can be estimated from the projected shipments of products containing the material, from planned material requirements, or from actual usage.

As with turnover, this ratio measures overall performance in improving operations. The lower the better. A wide range of numbers for similar classes of materials shows imbalance clearly. Ratios that persist at one value or grow steadily show where the flow of materials is bogging down. *A reasonable goal in most manufacturing companies is to halve the ratio annually.*

Actual Versus Scheduled Output

The sets of numbers defining the planned output of manufacturing operations are called master production schedules. Their development and use are covered in Chapters 4 and 5. They drive the detailed planning for individual products to obtain requirements for all resources. They reflect the introduction of new designs, procurement of materials and equipment, production in the plant, budgets, and all related activities. They experience changes from two sources: customers revising quantities, models, or delivery dates and significant internal failures to execute the plans.

Comparing actual output of each product to its master production schedule provides a fine overall measure of both sales and plant performance. Close liaison of sales personnel and customers will minimize late changes in requirements. Sound plans well executed are among the primary objectives of manufacturing firms. *Raising the percentage of successful completion halfway between current levels and 100% is a sound annual goal.*

The Production/Delivery Ratio

The numerator is the time a manufacturing company takes to procure materials and deliver its products to customers. The denominator is the time in which customers expect to receive products after they have placed orders for them with suppliers. Customary values of this ratio vary from 1.0 for restaurants to 100 or more for heavy machinery makers. It is appalling how few firms know their P/D ratios.

Any excess over 1.0 mandates that the supplier commit some resources to procuring and processing materials for customers before their needs are known specifically and must be forecasted. The farther ahead this is done, the greater will be the investment in resources and the risk of waste through forecast errors. *Strenuous efforts to reduce this ratio by a factor of 2 annually will be practicable and worthwhile.*

Number of Defects in Materials, Products, and Data

This is a measure of the quality of work and should be applied to both materials and information. All people directly handling material and data should be measured. Two measures are needed: defects generated by each person and defects passed along to the next user. The goal for the latter is zero; each person should be provided with some means for identifying defects and no excuses accepted for errors passed on. Materials are not absolutely uniform, mechanical equipment not completely reliable, and people not infallible, however, so some defects will result from processing. However, *zero defects is an achievable goal in screening materials and information moved to someone else.*

Percent of Records with No Significant Errors

Self-evident is the need for reliable data to use in making sound evaluations of performance and decisions for changes. Some companies have quantitative measures of record accuracy for inventory balances, fewer measure bills of material accuracy, and practically none can state a number for the accuracy of any other record.

The ways to detect and eliminate the causes of errors in records are well known and tested. A full explanation will be found in my Applications book (Bibl. 19). They work. Several concepts, all fallacies, account for the widespread failure to use them. Conventional wisdom holds that it is a massive, expensive task to eliminate errors, the costs will be excessive, it is unlikely to be successful because people will always make mistakes and tangible benefits will be small. None of these is true.

The value of improving data integrity is far higher than most managers believe. It is often the best profit improvement program a company can undertake; the tangible benefits far exceed the costs. Even if this were not so, it would be mandatory to find effective ways to improve data integrity if companies are to become and remain world-class competitors.

Present levels of accuracy are appallingly low in most firms and must be improved immediately. *The goal must be to cut the number of errors in half every six months*. The urgency of this cannot be exaggerated. The major impediment is the fallacious beliefs of managers cited above; this can be removed only by education.

Manufacturing Cycle Times

Some specific sequence of tasks, called the critical path—including designing, planning, procurement, production, testing, packaging, and shipment—determines the minimum time required to manufacture a product. This is the cycle time, the P in the P/D ratio discussed in this section. Brief analyses for product families will yield a number sufficiently accurate for management purposes. *A standing goal should be to reduce this cycle time by at least one-half every year.*

The technique is similar to that for cutting inventory—find where materials or information are sitting idle and get them moving. A work plan like Figure 7–6 can be developed easily (precision is not needed) to show "stalled" activities. Estimates of the amount of work present in major work areas like those listed in Figure 7–6 provide the baselines to attack.

Small teams of people working in each area, helped by a few staff specialists, can quickly identify the causes of delays. If these causes lie within their own area, they can be corrected fast; if they involve other functions, joint meetings of two or more cycle-reduction teams can resolve them. Using this approach, a manufacturer of preengineered, prefabricated steel buildings cut cycle times, *including design engineering,* from more than four months to less than three weeks.

Activity	Days Required
Order Entry, Including Credit Check	2
Order Editing	5
Release to Production	10
Receiving	2
Incoming Inspection	5
Raw Material Stores	20
Fabrication of Components	20
Component Stores	20
Kitting Components for Assembly	10
Final Assembly	15
Test and Repair	5
Packaging	2
Finished Goods Stores	20
Shipping	3
Invoicing, Including Followup	5

Total Cycle Time = 144

Figure 7–6 Manufacturing Cycle Time Elements

Percent of Real Work in Cycle Times

This measures the "fat" in cycle times, time when no value is being added. Typically, real work rarely takes 20% of total cycle time; often it is below 5%. Figure 7–7 shows a sequence of activities starting (at the bottom) with procurement of some raw material and then processing through several stages of production resulting in some finished product. The bars represent the planned lead times for each stage. The shaded section of each bar shows the working portion of the lead time—including moving the materials into the work area, setting up equipment, and processing. As shown, during the bulk of the time no value is being added to materials. Opportunities for improvement in the cycle time are enormous. Unfortunately, few people in manufacturing companies have taken the time to investigate what fraction of the planned time is occupied with real work. This measure will amaze most people.

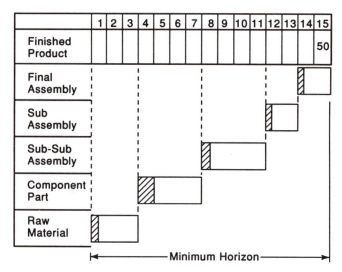

Figure 7-7 Stacked Lead Times

Attacks on delays reduce overhead costs and capital investment by significant amounts and generate many other benefits (see Chapter 6). They require relatively small efforts and expenditures to succeed. The catalyst to facilitate the management process of speeding up the manufacturing process is a clear recognition of the feasibility and desirability of doing it. *Making a decision to begin is harder than doing it.*

Productivity

The simplest way to measure overall productivity in any manufacturing company uses total value of products shipped and total hours worked by all employees using the formula:

Productivity = Products Shipped / Hours Worked

Any improvement in performance of one or two groups of people is pure waste if this ratio remains the same. Some gains could be claimed if reductions in high-pay people more than offset additions of low-pay ones; the opposite is much more likely. Shipping a larger proportion of high–profit margin products would be a gain not reflected in this ratio. Productivity measured in this simplistic way *should be improved by at least 5% per year in well-run companies and 10% in others.*

Among American executives and managers there is a perception that productivity increases require better motivation of workers and/or more mechanization and automation of their work. While both of these approaches are effective, the quickest and least expensive way to increase productivity is to eliminate some of the required tasks. In my experience with many companies, this elimination of unnecessary work and the benefits of sound planning and control have raised the productivity of direct workers by a minimum of 10% and as much as 50% and more. Compare these to the national average increases of 2–3%.

This ending of unneeded tasks cannot be done for indirect, clerical, or knowledge workers by working within one department or function; much of the work these people have to do is caused by others outside their function. A global view of activities within the whole company can yield productivity increases of from 25 to 60% since this area has been given a little attention.

Study of the activities of a firm's people influenced by suppliers and customers is needed to increase these people's productivity. There is very little written on this subject, but I am convinced that the opportunities here are great also.

Number of Certified Suppliers

The value of and techniques for establishing long-term partnerships with carefully selected suppliers is covered in Chapter 6. The techniques apply to those furnishing both materials and services. It is unlikely that any manufacturing company will ever have all suppliers certified, but heavy pressure must be exerted to *certify the 20% which furnish 80% of the value of purchased goods and services. This can and should be achieved in less than two years.*

Number of Components in Each Product

Many facets of plant operations are improved when the numbers of parts in products is reduced. Material and labor costs come down; overhead costs related to procurement, processing, planning, and control are lessened; quality problems are fewer; and less capital is invested in inventory. This number measures one of the major factors in the manufacturability of designs. *The goal of design engineering should be to reduce it by at least 20% each year.* Some ways to do this are presented in Chapter 6.

Number of Bottleneck Work Areas

Bottlenecks—machines or people in work areas incapable of processing the total amount of materials required to execute the plans—are intolerable. There is no problem more damaging in its effects. Bottleneck work areas are detected by measuring the total actual throughput and comparing it to the planned total in each time period. An allowance for unplanned work (i.e., unexpected scrap or rework, recovery from record errors) should be included in the plan. The presence of a bottleneck is not necessarily the fault of production; engineering design changes and "surprise" customer changes also cause them. *The acceptable number of bottlenecks is zero and fast action to break them is mandatory.*

Number of Schedules Missed

A narrow tolerance, one or two days, should be allowed before a missed schedule is recorded in production areas. This tolerance may be wider on shipments to customers if acceptable to them. As operations are brought under tighter control, these tolerances should be reduced. *An ultimate goal of zero percent tolerance on customer orders is realistic.*

The performance measures presented here are the most important for use by top management in directing and controlling plant operations. None requires a powerful, sophisticated computer- based system; the data are available already in existing systems in most companies. These measures are for use not only by operations people; their effects are so pervasive that executives and high-level managers should use them also.

SPECIFIC MEASURES FOR FUNCTIONS

In addition to the financial and physical performance measures presented here, several others are pertinent to the activities of organizational groups. Here are some to consider, with a proviso for continual improvement:

Marketing and Sales

Customer demand forecast accuracy— set minimum; aim to improve continually.
Range of variation of product family demand—strive to halve each year.
Contract bidding success rate—20% higher each year.
Number of products with low sales—set minimum percent of total sales.
Number of customer-desired order changes—goal = zero.
Number of surprises by customers— one is too many.
Number of surprises by competitors— one is too many.
Characteristics of firm's image with customers—based on interviews with a good sample cross section.

Design Engineering

Number of levels in bills of material—10% less each year.
Level of bills of material where model becomes unique—top level (finished product) is best.

Number of components in each product—10% less each year.

Percent of common components among product families—10% more each year.

Percent standard, commercial materials—20% more each year.

Number of different processes needed—5% less each year.

Number of corrective engineering changes issued—zero is the goal.

Number of changes from "as designed" to "as made"—zero is the goal.

Time from design assignment to production release—50% less each year.

Number of new product technologies evaluated—set some acceptable minimum.

"Customer" satisfaction with service—zero is goal for complaints from other departments served.

Process Engineering

Setup time—single digits of minutes.

Production cycle times—50% less each year.

Balance among operations on families of items—less than 2% imbalance.

Tooling and fixtures availability and reliability—zero production delays.

Investment in preproduction equipment (tooling, gages, fixtures, test equipment)—15% annual reduction by combining and standardizing.

Production plant floor space requirements—reduce by 15% annually for existing products.

Number of new process technologies evaluated—set some acceptable minimum.

Percent time serving other functions—increasing steadily, particularly for design and production.

"Customer" satisfaction with service—no complaints.

Plant Engineering and Maintenance

Percent reduction in energy consumption—minimum of 10% annually.

Mean time between equipment failures— annual increase of 25%.
Interruptions to production from equipment failure—50% reduction annually.

Interruptions to production from loss of utilities— one per year for each utility.

Integrity and availability of plant layout information—zero significant defects in computer file data.

Investment in maintenance and repair supplies—25% cut each year.

Number of violations of safety, pollution, and other regulations— one is too many.

Cost Accounting

Number of unique accounting transactions (not using physical input or not used by operations people)—limit to legitimate external requirements.

Days delay of reports after period close—allow two.

Number of obsolete reports still issued— eliminate any with two or less users.

"Customer" satisfaction with service—aim for no complaints from internal departments.

ESSENCE OF CONTROL

The essence of control consists of

* Valid plans, capable of being executed.
* Timely, accurate feedback comparing planned with actual performance.
* Measures of performance focusing peoples' attention on the important variables.
* Preset tolerances to highlight significant variances.
* Exception reports to initiate corrective actions.
* Thorough, knowledgeable analyses of alternatives to determine the proper responses.
* Prompt actions to get back on plan or revise it.
* Follow-up to ensure successful completion of actions or necessary changes.

The right performance measures will focus management's attention on the important problems needing solutions. Not knowing how to improve operations and clean up the environments of their plants, many executives attempt to tighten controls with more complex, detailed, and sophisticated cost accounting systems. New and powerful computer-based systems have tempted managers to collect and process more data in such systems in the mistaken belief that this would improve control. Such practices are now seen to be archaic at best, and obsolete, at worst.

Getting more precise numbers for the same old performance measures is futile. A few good approximations of key variables will be much more useful.

Trends, not absolute values, of performance measures provide key information. Also needed are measures of the total performance of a business based on a broader view than that provided by the conventional numbers. Among these, which cannot be handled by conventional accounting, are:

1. Market share, particularly in the markets important to the company's future.
2. Liquidity, indicating the firm's ability to finance growth through cash flow rather than borrowing.
3. Profitability, based on operations, not sales of assets or innovative accounting practices.
4. Innovation, indicating ability to develop and produce new products or services for future growth and health.

John Burbidge devoted a full chapter in his text, *Principles of Production Control*, (Bibl. 3) to "parameters of production," which he defined in three categories:

* Commercial: selling price, credit terms, and discounts
* Flow: batch quantity and frequency, product output, and ordering phase
* Technological: design, planning, layout, and organization

He pointed out the interactions of these parameters with the conventional performance measures and described the direction of change in the latter induced by changes in the former. Few nonmanufacturing managers understand these relationships.

A serious handicap in building a production organization flexible and resourceful enough to support dynamic marketing efforts is the long-time bias of executives to use rigorous cost-benefit analyses in measuring its performance. This is never done for engineering, sales, and marketing programs and people, where intangible factors carry some weight. The full potential of manufacturing plants as strategic weapons will not be realized until intangible factors, other than those amenable to detailed cost-benefit analyses, are given some weight in evaluating production also.

Performance measures are much more than standards to measure people—they are the means to communicate desired objectives. Management must set challenging goals for the right activities if they desire really significant progress. These goals must force actions to do more than improve the efficiency of current activities; they must move people to work harder on the right things, find better ways to do what must be done, identify unnecessary activities, and eliminate them.

It is clear that operating management needs information not available in conventional accounting systems and control reports. The first step in getting this is to identify the primary measures of performance needed to run operations. These are considerably different from those used currently in most companies, as has been shown in this chapter.

The next step is to put the new measures into practice. Both steps require reeducation of executives and managers on how manufacturing can and should be directed and controlled. This will be done only when executives and managers recognize that they need such education and demand it. This book is written to stimulate such a demand before it is too late for both the companies and our national economy.

CHAPTER 8

Manufacturing in the Future

Survival requires a new way of life—delighting customers, strengthening associates, and outstepping competitors.

SUMMARY

Four reasons account for failure of U.S. companies to compete successfully: first, problems many foreign firms do not have; second, markets with biased rules; third, scarce and expensive capital; and fourth, lack of qualified top management. Correcting the last will bring the best results the fastest.

Many fallacies handicap efforts to make the required changes. Media people, political leaders, and many executives think that the U.S. economy is strong; professional managers are corrupt, at worst, and inept, at best; U.S. productivity still leads the world; service businesses can replace industry; a low value dollar is needed; financial manipulations benefit industry; and Pacific Rim manufacturers are unbeatable.

Management faces two urgent tasks: getting its own house in order and becoming effective in spreading the message of the dangers to and needs of industry. While the economic failures of socialism and communism opened up vast opportunities for U.S. manufacturers, environmental concerns added heavy burdens to industry. Changing from conservative, risk-aversion approaches to aggressive entrepreneurial risk acceptance requires a cultural change which reverses many popular conceptions.

Key strategies for the future include continuous education of all employees, viewing workers as a valuable resource rather than a commodity, smoothing out and speeding up material and information flows, increasing the productivity of capital, and insisting on unending improvement in the quality of everything. Other needed strategies are streamlining all processes, eliminating layers of organization, harnessing computer technology effectively, and moving to develop new technology breakthroughs quickly. It is not too late to return industry to its former healthy condition, but time, the most important resource, is running out. Opportunities will be very challenging but highly rewarding for those firms able to leapfrog competitors. All must fight not just to win but to survive.

THE SITUATION TODAY

Many apparently impregnable firms have disappeared, strong companies are having difficulty competing domestically, and international competitors have been steadily pushing U.S. companies out of world markets. Chapter 2 cited four important reasons for U.S. firms' failure to compete successfully at home and abroad:

1. Problems competitors do not have:
   a. Government hindrance and neglect
   b. Antagonistic labor unions
2. Market conditions very biased against U.S. firms
3. Expensive capital and focus on short-term profits
4. Lack of fully qualified top-level management

This book deals primarily with the fourth. It presents a first law, fundamental principles, useful techniques, and ways to apply them. It covers what executives need to know and to do to control manufacturing companies effectively.

Short treatment in this book of the first three factors does not imply that executives of industrial firms cannot and should not make significant efforts to correct these also. They can and must speak out, write, and act far more forcefully in the future than they have in the past to promote actions needed to restore the economy to health. Top-level managers have defaulted on their responsibility to present the importance of a sound economy strongly and clearly to society and to the legislative and administrative branches of government.

Even an astigmatic government like ours, unable to focus on the basic needs of a healthy manufacturing industry, must soon see that world political leadership, military protection against the crazies of the world, foreign aid, and massive domestic programs depend on generation of sufficient wealth. Manufacturing is the largest source of such wealth; agriculture and the extraction industries are smaller contributors.

Manufacturing also accounts for the bulk of our exports and is our only hope for balanced trade without a dramatic lowering of living standards.

It is probably too much to expect government to recognize now the prime importance of fostering individual savings to increase capital availability and of promoting capital investment in manufacturing through favorable tax treatment of capital gains and stock dividends. It is to be hoped, however, that extreme pressure for a more balanced federal budget will reduce some of the burden of uneconomic social and agricultural programs which literally aggravate the situations they are designed to cure.

The power and influence of labor unions are declining rapidly. Faced with the reality of potential business failure, most unions lower their demands and cooperate with management in the development of more competitive operations. The intransigent, arrogant, antagonistic labor leaders and their unions, typified by the airline mechanics and pilots, like the dinosaurs, are doomed to extinction. It is a pity that they will take some unfortunate companies with them.

Government agencies need to realize that U.S. manufacturing firms need their help in getting a level playing field in international markets. This does not mean direct financial assistance to manufacturing companies in trouble nor does it require protective tariffs and restrictive import regulations. What is needed first is a recognition of the importance to national defense and a sound economy of certain key industries (e.g., machine tools, aircraft, semiconductors, and computers) so that these and other vital technologies are not traded away to foreign competitors for short-term political or military gains.

The second need, equally important, is for strong negotiations with our trading partners to ensure that U.S. manufacturers have as open access to their markets as their firms have to ours. While some good progress has been made, this effort must continue. After agreeing in many conferences to open their markets, the Japanese have been ingenious in denying admission of U.S. products while theirs enjoy unrestricted access to ours. The full depth and breadth of this subject are covered well in Clyde Prestowitz's book, *Trading Places* (Bibl. 23).

The harmful effects on manufacturing of financial manipulations are discussed in Chapter 2. Antagonistic takeovers (and protective measures to fight them), leveraged buyouts, mergers, acquisitions, and spinoffs all siphon off large amounts of capital from investments needed to improve operations. Research and development funds are scarce and expensive. Heavy debt handicaps many companies' ability to compete successfully. Financial markets' requirements for short-term profits divert firms from actions with long term benefits. Like trade barriers, the contrast between Japanese and U.S. practices is startling. There is little that executives in individual companies can do about this; the help of economists and government is needed.

Company executives can do much to help their firms, starting with *becoming fully qualified to run them properly*. In his entertaining and instructive booklet, "So You Want to Be a Manager?" (Bibl. 2), Francis Bridges identified three types of people: those who make things happen, those who watch things happen and those—the overwhelming majority— who have no clear idea of what is happening. This classification applies to executives in manufacturing companies.

Too many underqualified executives have blamed their company's troubles on high direct labor and material costs. Their solution has been to buy materials and have work done in low–labor cost countries. Ignored have been the additional overhead and capital costs and the danger of putting someone else in their business through the inevitable transfer of technologies.

It is obvious in many industries that the elimination of all direct labor costs would still leave many U.S. firms noncompetitive. Conventional management wisdom would advocate selling off such operations at whatever price could be obtained to "cut the losses." Most such companies could be restored to financial health by operating them as they should and could be run by managers knowledgeable of sound manufacturing practices.

There are numerous examples in many industries proving that this can be done. In its cover story in the April 1989 issue, *Modern Materials Handling* presented AT&T's experience at its Shreveport, Louisiana, plant. Called the Shreveport Advantage, the program was initiated to try to avoid closing the plant. It included teaching workers how to be better team players in the manufacturing processes they operated, improving material flow, reduction of waste, and elimination of no-value-added operations. Its goal was continuous flow and focused factories from suppliers to customers.

Benefits after three years include reduction in defects to a few parts per million, large cuts in operating costs, over 75% reduction in inventory, faster movement of smaller lots from suppliers through the plant, shorter delivery cycle times, and receipt of the U.S. Senate's Productivity Award. Far from over, the program is still generating improvements. This is a fine example of the soundness and effectivity of the actions recommended in this book.

It is true that foreign competitors have some political and labor union advantages; these may never be overcome. But *they do fundamental things better*—they work more like a team, they've learned their trades better, and they work harder and longer. In particular, they pay more attention to doing basic things well—improving quality, keeping accurate records, eliminating problems, and cutting lead times. They invented none of these concepts, but they really work hard implementing them.

COMMON FALLACIES

As covered in Chapter 1, the manufacturing environment is characterized by masses of details and multitudes of problems. Preoccupation with this plethora of facts and factors has bewildered many people who have attempted unsuccessfully to comprehend and cope with them. The trick is to see, in this welter of confusion, the fundamental nature of the manufacturing process and to learn the basic principles by which it is governed. Thirty of these have been presented and explained in this book.

None of these is complex and difficult to understand. What does complicate the task of understanding how manufacturing can and should be run are many fallacies commonly accepted as truth; some of these were debunked in Chapter 2. Unlearning these is much more difficult than learning the right ways. Here are some more commonly held notions which are wrong:

U.S. Economy Is Strong

The consensus among many people in both government and nongovernment circles is that the U.S. economy is mature and healthy, certainly not in need of government assistance and protection from foreign competition. The loss of whole industries is blamed primarily on "poor management." This myth has diverted the attention of people who should be engaged in taking action from many needed changes in government-industry and foreign trade relations.

Professional Managers Are Unprincipled

While entrepreneurs like Steve Jobs, Ross Perot, and Ray Kroc are respected, professional managers like Harold Geneen, Roger Smith, and even Lee Iococca are viewed as more villainous than heroic. Publicity about professional managers focuses mainly on excessively high salaries, golden parachutes, and heartless plant closings and layoffs. The executives' dynamic, aggressive role in generating real wealth is viewed as evidence of personal greed.

There is just enough truth in these beliefs to make them very difficult to challenge but little study is needed to show that they are largely false. With very rare exceptions, the managers I have met and worked with in hundreds of companies are hardworking, sincere, ethical people struggling to cope with heavy responsibilities. In two of these responsibilities, however, management of manufacturing companies has failed badly: to respond properly to competition and to be effective ambassadors carrying the message of the true nature and objectives of manufacturing.

Poor Management Is the Principal Cause of U.S. Decline

Many blame losing whole industries primarily on underqualified managers, but this is only one factor. The burdens of taxes and governmental regulations in the United States far exceed those of many foreign competitors. Their home governments assist them in many ways and view their role as wealth generators positively rather than antagonistically and punitively. U.S. trade policies are determined more by political and military considerations than by economic concerns.

Several key industries—semiconductor, computer, communications equipment, and military electronics equipment makers, for example—are essential to bo''. defense and the overall economy. They need government help to survive. Some few companies will need, as Harley-Davidson did, protective tariffs *for a very limited period during which they must become competitive.* That this will be slow in coming is a classic understatement. Since tariffs favor a few producers more than many consumers, politicians have a built in bias against them. Emotional references to the importance of free markets clouds the real issues.

More helpful would be relaxation of antitrust laws to permit groups of companies in some industries (supercomputers and high-resolution television, for example) to pool research and development work and share manufacturing technology information. More effective help from the U.S. government is needed to ensure level playing fields for both domestic and foreign producers.

U.S. Productivity Still Leads the World

Some optimists take hope in the fact that U.S. productivity still leads that of other industrial countries. In 1988, compared to American workers' output, the French produced 86%, West Germans 81%, British and Japanese 72%, and South Koreans only 40%. It is true also that U.S. manufacturing productivity rose an average of 3.3% from 1979 to 1988, a higher rate than France and West Germany achieved.

The optimists ignore the 5.8% growth rate in Japan and the 4.7% in Britain; they follow the advice of that famous baseball player, Satchel Page, "Don't look back; somethin' might be gainin' on you." Since this race has no short-term end, those gaining on the field will overtake the leaders if they don't wake up very soon.

Service Industries Will Replace Manufacturing

Many have concluded that our best course of action is to give up manufacturing (except for a few undefined high-technology products)

and to become more service oriented. Those who believe service industries are the hope of the future cite employment in business slowdowns
in 1986 and 1989. In both, sluggishness in the manufacturing sector was
offset by a buoyant service sector which provided employment for record
numbers of people.

The lawyers who direct our political destinies, the economists and
financiers who dominate our financial economy, and the educators who
develop our youth all seem to agree. But they are wrong. They ignore
important factors determining our standard of living, they lack the
wisdom and courage to oppose those who want quick, easy solutions, and
they do not begin to understand manufacturing.

Unfortunately, two vital factors make the transition from a manufacturing to a service economy undesirable: service industries create no
real wealth, and the earnings of their workers average less than 80% of
those of manufacturing. The inevitable result of such a transition in any
country will be a lowering in the standard of living for all of its people.
Add to these the increasing investment in the "information society" for
expensive data processing and transmission equipment and the very low
productivity of the people using it, and the transition from manufacturing
to service industries becomes even less viable.

Low Value Dollar Is Needed

Economists and financiers see the value of the U.S. dollar in foreign
exchange as critical, influencing interest rates, foreign currency move-
ments, and exports of goods and services. The U.S. budget deficit domi-
nates their thinking, although it is a smaller portion of gross national
product here than in many other countries. Of the two ways to reduce it,
they see only increased revenues.

They are joined by politicians who fear loss of power if government
expenditures are reduced for their constituents' favorite causes. In spite
of the beneficial effects of lower taxes on the economy, demonstrated
strongly in the 1980s, both groups ignore (if they even know) the effects
of added burdens on manufacturing from the actions they advocate.

Financial Games Are Beneficial

With the avowed purpose of strengthening weak firms, raiders and
takeover artists play games with high financial stakes, trading in whole
corporations and component firms. They know how to use junk bonds,
leveraged buyouts, and stockholder greed to buy and sell companies.
Unfortunately, they do not understand how to make their own companies
perform better. With baser intentions, some executives of large corporations are motivated more by their desires for personal wealth and power

than by their concern for the health and welfare of their companies. A little knowledge is a bad thing.

A classic example of what can be done by those who know how is the Smith-Corona Division of SCM. From 1981 to 1985, Smith-Corona had been a losing business. In 1984, G. Lee Thompson was recruited to turn it around. Here's what he did:

* Directed redesign of the product line to

    1. Exceed or at least match features of competitors—many word-processor features were included.
    2. Reduce the number of components—electric typewriters had 4,000 parts, early electronic machines had 1,700, the new SCM models had only 700.

* Pulled back all but highly labor-intensive (15% of total) work from foreign suppliers.
* Challenged U.S. workers to improve productivity—they quadrupled their productivity in the 1985–1986 period.
* Reduced overall labor costs by 60%.
* Increased market share from 30% to 40% and expect to continue to take more.
* Turned the company from a long-term loser to a highly profitable, world-class competitor.

Thompson knew how manufacturing operations could be improved and attacked fundamental problems vigorously. Instead of spinning off the losing typewriter division, SCM has kept it and put other less profitable operations on the block. Too bad they could not find someone to turn them around like SCM.

Japanese Manufacturers Are Unbeatable

Frequent references are made in U.S. media to Japanese cultural advantages against which U.S. firms cannot expect to compete successfully. A little analysis shows the fallacies in this thinking:

* U.S. plants have processing equipment and technologies equal to or better than Japanese. The latter are better at improving the use of such equipment.
* U.S. workers are equal to or better than Japanese in developing and applying innovation. They are lacking in education in basic subjects.
* U.S. has superior infrastructure, space, and natural resources. The Japanese waste less.
* U.S. management seeks quick solutions and rewards. The Japanese are patient and dogged in making progress.

The Japanese learned from the United States most of what now makes them tough competitors. We can take from them the lessons which will help us regain our previous competitive lead.

URGENT TASKS FOR EXECUTIVES

What will it take to get more universal recognition of the dangers from further attrition of our manufacturing base and the need for more teamwork among the important parties influencing manufacturing's future? A pessimist would say, "A miracle." Certainly the loss of jobs; a high, unfavorable balance of trade; and the increasing dependence on foreign sources for key components and products are very clear indicators of the results of loss of competitiveness and compelling reasons for regaining it.

Manufacturing company executives and managers have two jobs which need doing urgently: getting their own houses in better order and spreading widely the message of danger and urgency. It would be a mistake for them to start telling politicians, lawyers, financiers, and the media the error of their ways. They can make their case to the people whose inherent good sense has been evident in our society over time and whose power has been seen clearly recently, even in communist and socialist countries.

Like the politicians and media, few educators have shown that they have a sound understanding of our economic system and even fewer seem able to teach it to our general population. This book does not attempt this challenging job. More managers speaking out on the importance of manufacturing as well as showing how well they can run their companies are the most potent tools to get this job done. The future will need many such disciples.

The evident economic failure of socialism and communism has opened up new markets in a multitude of Central and South American, African, Asian, and Eastern European countries formerly closed to Western manufacturers. The economic integration of Western European countries has resulted in the world's largest single market. These have changed manufacturing forever but too many of the executives directing U.S. companies have failed to realize this. Of those who do, too few comprehend fully how to cope with the new realities.

Management will not be able to give undivided attention to taking advantage of these opportunities, however. The problems of pollution and degradation of the environment are approaching a critical stage. Planet Earth is finite and fragile. Environmental concerns have become as important to Americans as crime and drugs and more so than AIDS, nuclear war, and abortion. Instead of generalized feelings about some perceived but distant problem, the greatest concern of many individuals now is about their homes, neighborhoods, and planet Earth. The sources of pollution are fairly well identified but the seriousness of the problems and their solutions are still heatedly debated. Many health issues triggering extreme measures have turned out to be nonissues when more facts were known. As long ago as the 1950s, "laboratory tests" rated cranberries carcinogens; more recently, "scientific evidence" showed that Alar made apples dangerous to eat.

Conservationists and environmentalists, often uninhibited by facts, attempt with some success to force expensive and ill-considered solutions to such "problems." Acid rain and global warming are two examples. Industry is accused loudly of being the primary cause of global warming, air and water pollution, acid rain, human health hazards, and destruction of the environment. It is now recognized that others—city, state, and national governments; individuals; and even natural forces—are more serious offenders. Whatever the facts, industry must become a more responsible citizen and must carry its share of the burden of protection of people and their environment.

Determining its proper share is complex and depends on valid measures of environmental factors. Industry must assist government in determining these. Penalties for hazardous conditions must be severe but based on reason, not emotion, and must be effective in reducing hazards. This is easy to say but extremely difficult to do in the emotional, political arena which exists. Vocal industrial managers and supporters have a role to play.

Even-handed laws and regulations that treat all alike are not likely to result. Emotional, punitive approaches will aggravate the environmental problems and place unnecessary, damaging burdens on U.S. industry, already in trouble. Reasonable, practical solutions like umbrella standards and saleable vouchers will be ignored if the leaders in industry continue to abdicate their responsibilities as teachers and protagonists in the battle against degradation of the environment.

Within industry a very fundamental problem exists. Developing a culture in manufacturing companies to accept, handle, even love change will involve awakening an entrepreneurial spirit in almost everyone. This spirit thrives on change and accepts risks as inevitable in growth and improvement. The current corporate culture is exactly opposite; it strives primarily to avoid making mistakes; hence, it resists change, prefers to maintain the status quo, and demands in-depth analyses of many factors.

These slow down decision making and action while the world around is speeding up. Reversing these perceptions is possible, but *it must start with an edict from the top and be fostered at all organization levels every day.* The degree to which this is done will measure the real strength of a company to adapt to today's world.

Workers are now viewed in the most successful companies not as just a commodity but as a scarce and precious resource. The distinction between them and managers is disappearing. The more enlightened companies are providing an environment in which all employees can contribute more brain power and not be limited to work involving only muscle and bodily senses.

Shallow organization structures place more authority and responsibility on all people to make better decisions faster. The extremes of specialization are vanishing; machine operators are assuming maintenance, quality control, and scheduling duties, for example, while the "experts" in these are teaching them the tricks of their trades. Chapter 6 contains more on this topic. The potential benefits are enormous.

STRATEGIES FOR THE FUTURE

The first future strategy needed is

1. Make education of all employees a continuous effort.

The scope of the educational job is enormous. The changes needed to become world class competitors are fundamental and represent a new way of life. *The Wall Street Journal*, in its 1989 centennial edition, stated, "For most companies, nothing short of a philosophical break with the past will suffice."

Management must take the lead in developing the necessary educational programs to overcome the handicaps of the past and prepare all of their people for the future. The objectives of such programs must be to

* Impart more knowledge of what manufacturing is and what it does.
* Develop needed technical skills and abilities.
* Stimulate interest in self-improvement.
* Develop work practices which permit initiative and problem solving rather than rote performance.
* Provide understanding of relationships with others and demonstrate the need for teamwork.
* Communicate company policies, goals, and objectives.
* Enlist all employees in company improvement.

The need for education and improved understanding of manufacturing has never been more acute. In its 60th anniversary issue September 25, 1989, *Business Week* editors said, "The most pressing need is to increase our investment in human capital." While education is truly an investment, conventional accounting systems treat it as an expense, with immediate detrimental effects on profits. This as another example of serious problems caused by conventional accounting systems.

This can be no one-time, crash program. Motivation and understanding come in spurts; lack of continuous stimulation will result in early loss of the lessons. This was seen clearly in such fads as "zero defects" and "MRP II" programs. Continuously improving manufacturing performance is too important to risk backsliding. Workers' failure to learn well and in time will be catastrophic for a company and very damaging to the country's economy.

Failures in the public education of youth and the changing composition of the labor force make the task much more extensive and acute in the last decade of the twentieth and first of the twenty-first centuries. New immigrants from many countries, Hispanics, African-Americans, and poor whites will make up over 50% of the growth in the labor force. Lacking many of the basic skills of the older workers, these individuals will require extensive education to provide the skills and abilities needed for American firms to compete.

The difficulty of overcoming past practices and achieving a new way of life are illustrated in Harley-Davidson. This now famous motorcycle company, brought back from the brink of economic disaster, showed how American companies could compete successfully. They did the right things between 1983 and 1987. As a result of productivity improvements and cost reductions, however, the number of people on the payroll fell from 3,800 to 2,200.

Continuing efforts to improve performance threatened further cuts as demand for large motorcycles was flat. The union and workers criticized this sharply, accusing the company of not caring for workers. Evidently, the lessons of the recent past were not learned well. When crises went away, these people relapsed into the old "protect all workers against any layoffs" syndrome even if this threatens the firm's competitive position—and the jobs of most workers. Old beliefs die hard.

Overall, however, the smaller percentage of direct labor in factory costs, the larger investment in employee development and training and the realization of the great contribution workers can make to better company performance is leading to more stable employment in U.S. manufacturers. Workers are being viewed as long-term investments and not commodities to be rented for short periods. More union contracts contain job security clauses. Ironically, the fraction of workers in the United States enjoying de facto permanent employment is higher than in Japan where such guarantees are highly publicized.

The first law of manufacturing presented here implies clearly the second future strategy:

2. Achieve significant, continuous improvements in the performance of the business by attacking waste in all activities.

The process of doing this is not a fad, gimmick, or one-time program or project; not a collection of specific techniques; nor is it aimed at one part of the organization. It is a journey, not a goal, for everyone. Technicians and experts refer to it as "just-in-time" or "total quality control." It is the only way to become and remain a world-class competitor in global markets.

The most significant word in this principle is "continuous." Past efforts to improve performance of manufacturing companies have been intermittent, characterized by periodic massive programs of capital investment in automation, robotics, or new production machinery; by major profit improvement programs; or by attacks on excess inventory. Special projects, usually short-lived, are launched when some new buzzword is heard. The fabled victory of the tortoise over the hare illustrates the best way—steady, stubborn progress wins the race. *Stride, don't try to leap, to success.*

No type of manufacturing business, no products, no processes, and no customer or government restrictions prevent any company from applying this strategy to improving its operations. The reasons it has been used so seldom are not technical but emotional and conceptual. Companies don't believe it applies to them.

The third future strategy is equally clear:

3. Smooth out and speed up material and information flows.

This has been the main thrust of this book. It is clear now from the experiences of a multitude of companies in many countries that faster response to customers' needs is as important in manufacturing as in transportation and communication. Companies which cannot produce faster than their competitors are in danger; those who are slower are doomed. Of all resources used in manufacturing, time is the worst to waste. It cannot be stored. No more can be bought at any cost. All have equal amounts. Wise users will lead their competitors in wasting less time.

A fourth strategy for the future will be difficult to get widely accepted. It states

4. Increase the productivity of capital.

Improvements in productivity of labor and machines are widely believed to require heavy influx of new capital in manufacturing plants. Such money is scarce in the United States and more expensive (over twice the cost of capital in Japan) than in competing countries where savings rates are higher and lenders more tolerant. *U.S. News & World Report*'s November 20, 1989 issue highlighted the problem in an article, "Lean Times Loom on the Factory Floor," which stated, "At a time when Japan and West Germany are pumping record sums into new factories and state-of-the-art equipment, U.S. industries intend to scale back dramatically on capital spending. While plunging profits leave managers little choice, their actions threaten to erode the nation's future competitiveness, perhaps permanently."

Ironically, there is plenty of idle capital in most plants. It is easily seen in the materials in stockrooms and warehouses and on plant floors. Ironically also, *the actions which reduce the need for wasteful inventories are at least as effective in improving productivity as new capital equipment and add rather than diminish profits.*

My book *Manufacturing Control: The Last Frontier for Profits* (Bibliography #18) opened with this statement, "If your company could buy a 'machine' which not only paid for itself in less than one year but also reduced your net assets, it would snap up this opportunity!" The machine referred to was a modern computer-based planning and control system. In the hands of qualified managers, such a system can help increase the productivity of labor and capital enormously, often much more than robotics and automation and new capital-intensive machinery.

A fifth strategy for the future relates to quality

5. Work continuously to improve the quality of output of every business activity.

This strategy embraces much more than a company's products. It includes all materials and information processed or generated by the people in all parts of the organization. To emphasize the importance of better quality to U.S. manufacturers, the Department of Commerce instituted in 1988 the Malcolm Baldrige National Quality Award "to recognize quality achievements" and to "publicize quality strategies" of U.S. firms in three categories of industry. In the first two years, Motorola, Xerox, Eastman Kodak, Globe Metallurgical, and Milliken were among the winners. Whether these awards will have the desired effect of focusing the attention of management on quality improvements is not yet clear.

The winners, predictably, have been capitalizing on the advertising benefits. Some of the media, with characteristic misdirection, have been publicizing this aspect of public relations hype and the large clerical effort required to make application for the award. Managers could easily get the impression from such media coverage that the bulk of savings would be eaten up by application costs and conclude that there are better ways to advertise the company and its products and services.

This would be tragic. The Motorola story of the award is typical; here are some highlights:

* The program started in the cellular telephone division in 1981 when CEO Robert Galvin met with 80 corporate executives on quality problems and named a czar.
* Jack Germaine, the czar, set a goal of reducing defects by 90% by 1986.
* Design, quality control and manufacturing engineers, and production workers teamed up to find the basic causes of rejects and to eliminate them.
* Between 1981 and 1987, defects dropped from 1,000 per million to less than 100 per million, beating the goal.
* In 1987 Galvin visited customers to talk quality and set a goal of another reduction in defects to 3.4 defects per million (the so-called Six Sigma program) by 1992—now well on its way to achievement.
* Suppliers are being "invited" to join the "crusade."
* Employee training expenditures rose to $100 million/year.
* Motorola 1988 profits were a record $445 million; costs of production dropped $250 million.

Robert Galvin's comment summed up the most important lesson Motorola learned, "We'd always assumed you could get only so close, but we came to the conclusion that we human beings really can produce something that is virtually perfect." Has Zero Defects been reincarnated?

Manufacturing deals with many resources—capital, people, materials, machines, energy, time—all of which have great flexibility in application. This flexibility is reduced or even lost completely when these resources are used to produce some specific product. The sixth strategy statement repeats principle 5 in Chapter 1 because of its compelling importance:

6. Do not commit flexible resources to any specific item until the last possible moment.

The "last possible moment" is defined as the latest point in time that an action using resources can start and still result in completion on time to meet customers' needs. This principle recognizes that maximum efforts must be exerted to retain flexibility to respond to changes in market needs or production processes. It aims to delay execution of plans as long as possible so that actions are taken based more on true needs than plans.

The Wall Street Journal's 1989 Centennial Edition also listed four future strategies which are self-explanatory. It called these "critical":

7. Streamline factory processes to slash inventories, material costs, and production time.*

8. Pare management layers to force designers, engineers, production workers, and marketers to work as teams.*

9. Harness computer technology to make small batches of customized products at low cost.*

10. Pounce on breakthrough discoveries (like superconductivity) that will revolutionize entire businesses.*

Tom Watson, Sr., of IBM called the Great Depression of the 1930s and 1940s "...a golden decade full of risks and boldness." He saw clearly the importance of research and development investment to provide a fount of new products and technologies for a company's future growth. Interestingly, a large proportion of IBM sales have been in products they did not invent but developed and marketed successfully before competitors. Someone must make the R&D investment, however; this may be government, university, competitor, or company. This effort has been lagging in the United States and needs to be accelerated.

In *Thriving on Chaos* (Bibl. 14), Tom Peters stated the importance of manufacturing as a weapon in carrying out a company's strategies. He said, "Manufacturing must become a, if not the, primary marketing tool in the firm's arsenal. Quality, maintainability, responsiveness (length of lead time for delivery), flexibility, and the length of the innovation cycle...are all controlled by the factory."

HOPE FOR THE FUTURE

Ours has been a society of plenty—food, raw materials, energy, capital, space, and natural resources. We have been indicted as being wasteful and that charge is well deserved. But things have changed. Manufacturing in many industries now faces real crises. It is viewed by most people as the villain causing pollution, threatening the ecology, oppressors of labor, producers of shoddy goods, and promoters of crass materialism. It is no longer recognized as the main creator of real wealth and the economic foundation of all social progress. It is failing to enlist fresh, bright young minds and certainly not attracting the capital so necessary for growth.

American companies face a major uphill battle to regain the leading competitive role they had in the 1960s and 1970s. This fight will not be won just by working harder, neither can success be achieved by quick-fix programs, no matter how expensive. The activities of every group in the organization must be challenged, checked and changed. The price of the neglect and abuse of manufacturing over the last four decades must be paid and it is high. It will be a cultural revolution and everyone in manufacturing must take part.

The need is for a change in the way of life of each person and group. Faster, more flexible, and much more reliable service to customers must be a perennial goal. Close teamwork with suppliers must replace arm's-length, antagonistic relationships. The quality of all activities must be improved. Materials and information must move more smoothly and faster. Activities which add no value, only cost, must be eliminated. Raw material, work-in-process, component, and finished goods inventories are not assets; they must not be allowed to cover up problems which should be solved. In short, companies must meet all of their customers' needs, drive all costs downward, and utilize capital more efficiently.

Executives, managers, and workers in manufacturing firms must understand the fundamentals of manufacturing, its planning and control. They must apply the common, basic principles. They must solve the problems in their areas and improve their and others' productivity. Equally important, they must lead the effort to get people in our society and, through them, union leaders, politicians, educators, and others to understand the importance to all of a healthy, growing industry generating adequate amounts of real wealth.

Management always underestimates the potential benefits of getting manufacturing companies under good control by applying the approaches presented in this book. They believe that other actions—acquisitions, mergers, new markets, product lines, or machines or a powerful computer—will show better results. An appreciation of the "snowball rolling downhill" effect of improving operations, using the traditional financial performance measures, can be obtained from Figures 8–1, 8–2, 8–3, and 8–4.

Figure 8–1 shows a profit and loss statement; the numbers are in reasonable proportion for many firms and could be in millions of dollars but this is not important. Net sales (180) less cost of goods sold (100) yields a gross profit of 80 and net of 60. This is not too bad, but management wants better.

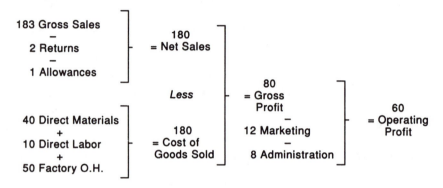

Figure 8–1 Profit and Loss Statement - Before

Figure 8–2 is the balance sheet giving the details of assets made up of inventories, plant and equipment, receivables, and cash. As in Figure 8–1, the numbers are reasonable and could be found in these proportions in many companies.

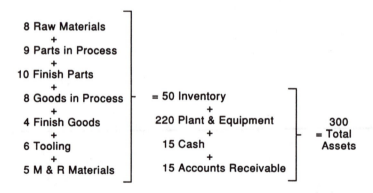

Figure 8–2 Balance Sheet - Before

Figure 8–3 shows how net operating profit could be improved by adopting modern planning and control practices and by improving execution using the approaches covered in this book. *All the changes indicated are conservative estimates.* Direct material costs were cut only 10%, direct labor and factory overhead costs were reduced by 20%, and product returns were eliminated by improved quality, giving a 33% profit improvement.

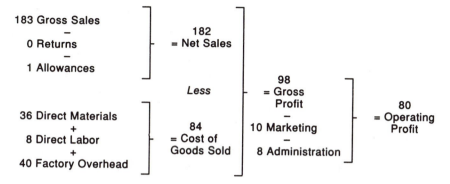

Figure 8–3   Profit and Loss Statement - After

The changes indicated in the new balance sheet shown in Figure 8–4 are also quite conservative. Inventory of raw materials down 25%, both parts and goods in process cut 50%, finished components reduced 25%, and finished products down 50% reflects good, but not uncommon, improvement. No credit has been taken for gains in plant and equipment (where existing facilities would undoubtedly have increased capacity) nor in accounts receivable (where improved deliveries should reduce them) both of which would probably occur.

The double-barreled impact of enhanced profits and reduced assets is seen clearly when return on asset ratios are calculated for both before and after cases.

$$\text{ROA (Before)} = 60/300 = 20\%$$

$$\text{ROA (After)} = 80/285 = 28\%$$

Figure 8–4   Balance Sheet - After

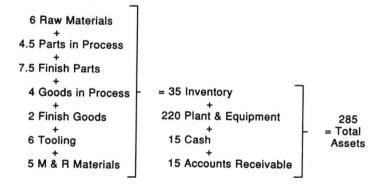

An interesting question for management is, *"What else can a company do which has the same potential to improve profits, capital use, and customer satisfaction, all at the same time?"*

While they are extremely effective and seem simple in concept, it is easy to underestimate the difficulty of applying these principles and techniques. Key managers see no need for them to take the time or make the effort to develop full understanding; they think they can safely leave such things to the experts. While the changes are simple in concept, they are hard to achieve and will never be realized without full participation by top management. They must work to perceive the extent and nature of the changes needed in people, products, and processes and to ensure that such changes come about.

Time is not only our most important resource, it is also our scarcest. Turning our economy around is extremely urgent if it is to be done successfully. It will require a massive job of motivation and education of executives, managers, and all people operating manufacturing firms. Most of these now are undereducated and overmanaged. Fully qualified people are our real assets, the only ones that appreciate in time. We need their brains far more than their muscles and five senses.

Opportunities for manufacturing businesses in the future will be orders of magnitude greater than those of the past. The reduction in military confrontation between the United States and the Soviet Union will permit diverting enormous amounts of capital from war materials to consumer products. The economic union of West European countries creates the largest single market in the world. The breakdown of totalitarian governments in Eastern Europe releases enormous demand for manufactured products. Asian, African, South American, and other developing countries markets have great potential for those firms which accept and know how to handle risk.

Aggressive companies recognize the real value of getting into markets first. Name and product recognition are important, of course, but even more so is getting the best local talent on their team. The risks are clear: unstable governments, lack of local infrastructure, obsolete plants, currency exchange limitations, and uncertain customers' preferences. Successful companies will do their homework thoroughly, studying the markets, politics, and other relevant factors; will commit limited amounts of resources, and will press for results but expect slow returns. Planning for the long range is the game; quick payoffs will be rare. The real balancing act will be moving quickly enough but not jumping too fast. Risk and reward will both be great.

It is literally incredible that a nation like ours with all the necessary ingredients for a healthy industrial economy should be falling upon such hard times. The United States has what it takes—the natural resources, the energy, the skilled and intelligent labor force, the capital, the transportation infrastructure and the large markets—for a successful industrial effort.

The keys to leapfrogging competition, each discussed in detail in earlier chapters, are:

* Educate to enhance people's skills and abilities.
* Smooth and speed up material and information flow.
* Shorten processing cycle times of all activities.
* Become more proactive than reactive.
* Mount continuous, relentless assaults on all wastes.
* Improve teamwork with suppliers and customers.

The future will be fertile or futile depending on the ability of top-level managers in the United States to redirect their efforts in operating manufacturing companies. Manufacturing businesses are not loosely knit confederations of marketing, engineering, finance, and manufacturing activities but are, with their suppliers and customers, a single entity needing a unified, integrated effort with all functions working closely together utilizing common strategies.

The United States must develop more top-level executives who understand the essence and fundamentals of manufacturing and can direct their teams of managers to develop worldwide competitive abilities. Understanding alone is not enough. The Bible states the need (James 2:17): "Faith by itself, if it has no works, is dead." We can watch our economic base continue to erode or we can fight our way back to the leadership we once enjoyed. It shall be as management wishes. Companies are no longer competing just to win but to survive.

Bibliography

1. Bell, D. "Five Dimensions of Post-Industrial Society." *Social Policy* (July–August 1973).
2. Bridges, F. C. *So You Want to Be a Manager.* Decatur, GA: ESM Books, 1984.
3. Burbidge, J. L. *The Principles of Production Control*, 3rd ed. London: MacDonald and Evans, 1971.
4. "Small Backlogs = Big Control." *Executive's Bulletin*. Bridgeport, CT: Bureau of Business Practice, 1965.
5. Fitzsimmons, J. A. and R. S. Sullivan. *Service Operations Management.* New York: McGraw-Hill, 1982.
6. Ford, Henry. *Today and Tomorrow*, reprint ed. Cambridge, MA: Productivity Press, 1988 (1926, Doubleday, Page & Company).
7. Geneen, H. *Managing.* Garden City, NY: Doubleday, 1984.
8. Gue, F. S. *Increased Profits Through Better Control of Work in Process.* Reston, VA: Reston, 1980.
9. Halberstam, D. *The Reckoning.* New York: Wm. Morrow, 1989.
10. Hall, R. W. *Attaining Manufacturing Excellence.* Homewood, IL: Dow Jones-Irwin/APICS Series, 1987.
11. Harris, F. W. *Operations and Cost*, Factory Management Series. Chicago: A. W. Shaw, 1915.

12. Johnson, H. T. "Activity-Based Information." *Target* (Assoc. for Mfg. Excellence, Chicago), Vol. 5, no. 1 (1989).

13. Peters, T. J., and R. H. Waterman. *In Search of Excellence*. New York: Harper & Row, 1982.

14. Peters, T. J. *Thriving on Chaos*. New York: Alfred A. Knopf, 1987.

15. Plossl, G. W. *Manufacturing Control: The Last Frontier for Profits*. Reston, VA: Reston, 1973.

16. Plossl, G. W. *Production & Inventory Control: Applications*. Marietta, GA: Geo. Plossl Educ. Services, 1983.

17. Plossl, G. W. *Just-in-Time: A Special Roundtable*. Marietta, GA: Geo. Plossl Educ. Services 1985.

18. Plossl, G. W. *Production & Inventory Control: Principles & Techniques*, 2nd ed. Englewood Cliffs, NJ: Prentice-Hall, 1985.

19. Plossl, G. W. *Effective Corporate Strategy in Manufacturing*. Marietta, GA: Geo. Plossl Educ. Services, 1986.

20. Plossl, G. W. "Throughput Time Control," *International Journal of Production Planning & Control*. London: Taylor & Francis, 1988.

21. Plossl, G. W. "Cost Accounting in Manufacturing: Dawn of a New Era." *Journal of Production Planning & Control*. London: Taylor & Francis, 1989.

22. Plossl, K. R. *Engineering for the Control of Manufacturing*. Englewood Cliffs, NJ: Prentice-Hall, 1987.

23. Prestowitz, C. V., Jr. *Trading Places*. New York: Basic Books, 1988.

24. Schonberger, R. J. *Japanese Manufacturing Techniques*. New York: Macmillan/Free Press, 1982.

25. Shingo, Shigao. "Study of Toyota Manufacturing System." Tokyo: Japan Management Association, 1981.

26. Skinner, Wickham. "Manufacturing—Missing Link in Corporate Strategy." *Harvard Business Review* (May–June 1969).

27. Taylor, S. G., et al. "Process Industry Production and Inventory Planning Framework, Production & Inventory Management." *Journal of APICS* (First Quarter 1981).

28. Wilson, R. H. "A Scientific Routine for Stock Control." *Harvard Business Review*, Vol. 13, no. 1 (1934).

Glossary of Terms

Active Inventory Raw material, work-in-process, or finished products which will be used or sold in the near future.

Actual Capacity A sustained rate of production throughput of a facility based upon recent actual performance (see also *Demonstrated Capacity*).

APICS (American Production and Inventory Control Society) A technical organization of individuals involved or interested in the field of manufacturing planning and control and related activities. It has affiliates (Canadian, CAPIC; British, BPICS; etc.) in many other countries.

Asset Management Planning and control of all activities related to the needs for and utilization of capital assets both fixed and working.

Augmenters Individuals whose activities contribute directly to increasing business' growth, profitability, and/or return on investment (examples: R&D, design engineering, marketing).

Automatic Rescheduling An MRP program in which the computer is allowed to change the due date on released orders just as it does on planned orders.

Backlog of Orders The number of all unfilled customer, manufacturing, or purchased orders (not necessarily late).

Backlog of Work The total of uncompleted work at a work center (not necessarily late) in product or work units.

Balanced Loading Releasing to a starting department or gateway work center a product mix suitable to develop a smooth flow in downstream secondary departments.

Balanced Operations Adjusting capacity among sequences of operations to permit processing a required amount of work without bottlenecks.

Batch Any order quantity that combines one or more known or forecast needs of the future into a single order.

Bill of Materials A listing of the components of an assembly, subassembly, or fabricated part.

Bookings Total The value of all customer orders received and entered but not shipped.

Bottlenecks Operations with too little capacity to handle the total work needed in the current time period.

Business Plan A projection of customer demand, production levels, costs, income, capital requirements, and other management data used for medium- and long-range planning of product families.

Buying Capacity Contracting to purchase a portion of a supplier's output without specifying details.

CAD See *Computer-Aided Design.*

CAE See *Computer-Aided Engineering.*

CAM See *Computer-Aided Manufacturing.*

CAPP See *Computer-Aided Project Planning.*

Capacity The amount of work a facility can perform in a period of time (see also *Actual, Planned,* and *Theoretical Capacity*).

Capacity Requirements Planning Determining the rate of input and/or output of work in a facility needed to support the master production schedule.

CFM See *Continuous Flow Manufacturing.*

Cell See *Flexible Machining Systems* and *Group Technology.*

Closed-Loop System A planning and control system in which feedback of data from actual activities is used to determine the need to revise the plan.

Common Parts Those component parts which are commonly used in two or more of a company's products or models.

Component An item listed in any bill of materials for a parent.

Computer-Aided Design Computer hardware and software for product design and drafting.

Computer-Aided Engineering Computer hardware and software for design, drafting, project planning, and business planning of engineering activities.

Computer-Aided Manufacturing Computer hardware and software for process planning, tooling, testing, and quality control.

Computer-Aided Project Planning Computer hardware and software for planning and controlling total projects.

Computer Integrated Manufacturing (CIM) A closed-loop manufacturing control system whose inputs are product requirements and concepts and outputs are finished products. The primary objective of the system is to assist design, analysis, and planning and control of production, materials, and processes.

Continuous Flow Manufacturing (CFM) Operations in which materials flow (almost) continuously through the necessary sequence of operations (work cell) although processing can be changed periodically to make a variety of products.

Continuous Production Uninterrupted production of the same or very similar items (as in a refinery).

Control Comparing execution with plans, finding significant deviations, and initiating corrective actions.

Control System One designed to monitor the output of a process, compare actual with planned data, and respond to deviations greater than a predetermined tolerance.

Cumulative Lead Time The largest sum of all of the planned lead times required to process raw materials through all operations into a finished product.

Cycle Time The total time between starting and finishing a product, including all work on components but not including procurement of purchased items.

Data Base Data needed in planning and control activities stored in flexible, expandable files for common use by all operating functions of a company.

Delivery Cycle The calendar time from the receipt of an order to the shipment of the material covered to the customer.

Demand Management The activities involved in planning for and handling all types of demand including customer, interplant, and branch warehouse orders.

Demonstrated Capacity The actual output rate of work centers or vendors usually measured in standard hours and averaged over several recent weeks.

Direct Labor Work by humans applied directly to production.

Distribution The activities including warehouse location studies, inventory planning and control, shipment to warehouses, and material handling involved in managing a company's inventory in branch warehouses and consigned stocks.

Documentation Written descriptions of formal systems and procedures (detailed for systems designers, generalized for users).

Economic Order Quantity The batch size to be purchased or made which minimizes the total of ordering and inventory carrying costs.

Engineering Change A formal revision of product specifications or designs to improve function, quality, or cost.

Execution Actions which convert plans into reality.

Expediting Speeding up an items progress through personal attention of an individual.

Facilities Planning The process of determining the type and quantity of buildings and production equipment required to support the business plan.

Family Several similar products in a product line or several similar components in a product.

Feedback Comparing actual performance against planned and reporting deviations greater than allowed tolerance.

Flexible Machining System (FMS) A group of numerical control machines linked by automated material handling equipment and directed by computer to produce a variety of items.

Flow Rate Number of units of production per unit of time, also called production rate.

Function A major organizational group responsible for one business function (i.e., engineering, marketing).

Functional Machine Center A group of machines performing identical or very similar functions (e.g., drilling).

Group Technology (GT) Arranging machines with different functions in a group to process a family of similar items.

Hard Data Facts on physical entities (i.e., inventories) and execution activities (assembly, shipping dates, etc.).

Hot List A shortage list prepared manually containing the immediate needs of manufacturing operations.

Indirect Labor Work by people supporting direct labor actions but difficult to assign directly to a part or product.

Integrated Planning System One designed to develop a common set of plans for different functions in a business.

Inventory Materials required for production, including raw materials, work-in-process, finished products, tooling, testing, supplies, and maintenance held internally or in external locations (warehouses or customers' plants).

Inventory Turnover The ratio of total sales to the inventory required to support these sales. Inventory value is always the cost; sales may be expressed in cost of goods sold, or gross or net sales dollars.

JIT See *Just-in-Time*.

Job Shop A facility producing nonrepetitive items such as custom-built, make-to-order products.

Just-in-Time (JIT) The philosophy which commits flexible resources (money, people, materials, machines, etc.) to a specific item only at the last possible moment. This is also referred to as the "zero inventory" philosophy and is implemented using techniques like Toyota's *Kanban* system.

Kanban A Japanese term meaning signboard or ticket. Used now commonly to refer to the Toyota "pull" system in which use of an item triggers its replenishment.

Lead Time Total time to procure or produce an item from release of order or schedule to availability for use.

Lead Time Syndrome The phenomenon resulting from increasing or decreasing planned lead times used in inventory replenishment techniques in a futile attempt to bring planned and actual values into agreement.

Load The amount of work waiting for processing at any facility (often confused with capacity).

MPS See *Master Production Schedule*.

MRP See *Material Requirements Planning*.

MRPII See *Manufacturing Resource Planning*.

Machine Center A group of similar machines treated as one unit when scheduling or loading.

Machine Utilization The ratio of actual time used to total scheduled operating time.

Manufacturing The industry and any business converting lower-valued materials to higher-valued products.

Manufacturing Resource Planning (MRPII) A misnomer for the formal manufacturing planning and control system, concerned with financial, engineering, production, and marketing activities as they relate to manufacturing. It ignores execution and control activities and has produced more confusion than benefits.

Master Production Schedule (MPS) Detailed schedules of amounts of products described by bills of material to be produced in specific time periods. It drives MRP and translates the master manufacturing plan into specific orders for needed components and also into capacity needs.

Material Requirements Planning (MRP) A time-phased priority planning and scheduling technique calculating component needs to support production schedules for parent items taking into account materials now available in stock as well as those on replenishment orders already released.

Master Scheduling The management process of developing, reviewing, and revising the master production schedules which drive the formal detailed planning system.

Open-Loop Systems without integrated feedback.

Ordering Cost The sum of the costs (not including direct labor and material) associated with ordering a batch of purchased or manufactured materials, including paperwork, machine setup, first piece inspection, and the like.

Pareto's Principle A statement by the Italian economist, Vilfredo Pareto, in the late 1800s recognizing that in any large group of similar items there are the "vital few," the most important, and the "trivial many," collectively of relatively little importance (the ABC inventory value classification system is based on this principle).

Pilot Lot The first production run of a manufactured item to prove the design and process capabilities and/or provide a quantity for a market test.

Planning Assigning numbers to future occurrences.

Planning Horizon The time periods in the future over which formal plans extend.

Product Families Groups of products similar in marketing or in manufacturing considerations.

Production The processing and direct support activities converting materials into products in manufacturing plants.

Production Control The activities and body of knowledge related to planning and controlling manufacturing operations.

Production Plan The high-level, long-range plan setting manufacturing rates for major product families recognizing material and capacity constraints and embodying management's policies on growth, stability, market share, customer service, and so on.

Production Rate See *Flow Rate*.

Production Types

Aerospace/Defense (Contract) Output of high-technology products, specific contracts subject to detailed audit.

Controlled Production (Regulated) Output of foods, medicines, or hazardous or toxic products subject to tight government regulations.

Intermittent (Batch, Job Lot) Make-to stock and make-to-order with frequent repeats of batches of any model.

Job Shop (Single Job Lot) Make-to-order, no repeats.

Process (Continuous Flow) Continuous output for long periods of bulk liquids, or granular or paste products in fixed flow paths.

Repetitive (Intermittent Flow) Steady-rate output, little variety.

Productivity The value (or amount) of useful output per unit of cost (or work) required to produce it.

Progress Payments Periodic payments by customers to suppliers for engineering, preproduction, procurement or production as work progresses on orders.

Pull System One in which replenishment is initiated by actual use of each item (see also *Kanban*).

Purchase Commitment The total value of materials on order with each supplier in a specific time period or over a given horizon of time.

Purchasing Capacity See *Buying Capacity*.

Push System One in which replenishment is initiated by planned, not actual, requirements for each item.

Quality Management A philosophy which states that quality should be managed for continual improvement and not simply controlled to maintain some acceptable level.

Queue Time Waiting periods or delays in movement of or work on paperwork or materials in production caused by the presence of several batches awaiting processing.

Scientific Inventory Control Application of theoretical, mathematical procedures such as economic order quantity and statistical safety stock calculations for the replenishment of an item's inventory.

Setup The activities to prepare a machine or work area to convert from making one item to making another.

Soft Data Planned data (budgets, order dates, etc.).

Staff Individuals whose activities add more cost than value to products (example: inspection and test).

Staging Physically gathering together the components needed to produce a parent item (usually done in a stockroom).

Subcontract Buying work (rather than just materials) from an outside source.

Subsystems Integral parts of a complete, integrated planning and control system such as purchasing, master scheduling, and others.

Supplier An external source of purchased goods and services.

System An integrated, formal set of files, procedures, transactions, and reports to aid people in their work.

TQC See *Total Quality Control*.

Throughput Time See *Cycle Time*.

Total Quality Control (TQC) A philosophy which extends the concepts of quality management into all activities of a manufacturing business.

Work-in-Process (WIP) Materials being worked on, ready for work, or moving between work centers in a manufacturing plant as contrasted to storeroom materials.

Work Order A broad term covering a means for authorizing all types of work in a manufacturing plant and scheduling it.

Index

A

Accounting:
  performance measures, 146
  practices lagging operations, 118
  problems with conventional, 160
  systems for financial use, 100
Accuracy of data, 89
Acid rain, 158
Aerospace/defense:
  compliance with DCAA
      regulations, 32
  problems, 14, 31
  subsystems, 84
  viewed as different, 30
Airline pilots' training vs.
      manufacturing managers, 109
American Production and Inventory
      Control Society, 6, 68, 77
Asset management, 42
AT&T Shreveport Plant, 152
Auto industry:
  problems from financial measures,
      24

Automatic control, 74
Automation:
  first test for, 92

B

Bad press for U.S. industry, 27
Balance Sheet example:
  after improvement, 167
  before improvement, 166
Balanced operations, 93
  improving, 94
Bell, Daniel, 30
Bill of labor, 78
Bills of material, 82
  as planning framework, 105
Book value of machinery, 100, 125
  poor decisions using, 125
Bottleneck work areas, 143
  effects of, 80
Branch warehouses, 102
  improving operations, 103
Burbidge, John, 147

Business plans, 55, 63
  questions answered, 63
  steps in making, 64
Business Week, 3, 16, 104, 160

C

Capacity:
  planning and control, 77
  requirements plan:
    detailed, 82
    only approximation, 82
    rough-cut, 78
  value of unused, 42
Capital funds in U. S.:
  why so expensive?, 133
Certified suppliers, 112
Charter of the business, 57
Chrysler Corporation, 106, 110
Classifications of manufacturing,
  46
Communism's failure, 157
Competition, leapfrogging, 169
Competitive strength
  important factors, 118
  restoring, 152, 156
Complex systems not required, 37
Complexity in manufacturing
  exaggerated, 6
Computer aided manufacturing
  (CAM), 83
Computer assisted design
  (CAD), 83
Computer assisted engineering
  (CAE), 83
Computer integrated manufacturing
  (CIM), 86
Conservationists, 158
Continuous processing, 8
Control:
  definition, 2, 13, 76
  essence of, 88, 146
  no one best way, 12
  report format, planned and actual
    shown, 128
  requirements, 48, 88
  systems, 74

  automatic, 75
  closed loop, 74
  necessary but not sufficient, 86
  open loop, 74
  steps in developing, 86
  why ineffective, 86
  theory, 74, 75
  timeliness of information, 90
Conventional wisdom:
  problems inevitable, 109
  professional managers can run
    any business, 122
  purchasing's role, 112
  record errors inevitable, 140
Core system elements, 77
Cost accounting performance
  measures, 146
Cultural changes needed, 96
  design engineering, 103
  entrepreneurial spirit, 158
  finance and accounting, 99
  maintenance and plant
    engineering, 113
  manufacturing engineering, 105
  marketing and sales, 101
  material planning and control,
    106
  production, 109
  purchasing, 112
  quality control, 108
  top management, 98
  warehouse and distribution, 102
Customer:
  delight, 41
  needs vs. wants, 61
  satisfaction, 40, 41
    requirements for, 41, 119
  service, 40
Customer/company relations, 41
Customer/supplier relations, 96,
  101, 112
Cycle time:
  arguments for short, 82
  attack teams, 96
  charting to reduce, 94
  Ford Dearborn plant, 110
  measuring, 110
  work plan to cut, 140

D

Data:
  hard, 89
  vs. information, 127
  soft, 89
Data files:
  common needed, 47
  quality, 48
Decision-making:
  with wrong numbers, 122
Defense Contract Audit Agency, 31
Delivery promises, 102
Deming, W. Edwards, 114
Design engineering:
  cultural changes, 103
  performance measures, 144
  primary task, 103
  strategies, 60, 162
Direct labor efficiency
      counterproductive, 122
Direct material costs:
  precise but inaccurate, 124
  total from foreign sources, 124
Drucker, Peter, 136

E

Eastman Kodak, 163
Economic order quantity, 29
Education:
  future strategy, 159
  as investment, 160
  objectives, 159
Effective control requirements, 89
Eliminating unnecessary activities,
    92
Environmental problems, 157
Environmentalists, 158
Equipment utilization, 42
Evidence of lack of control, 3
Exception reports, 91
Execution:
  definition, 13, 76
  purpose, 77
Executive tasks:

cultural changes, 98
get house in order, 157
getting qualified, 152
promote industry, 150, 157
strategies, 57, 159, 161
Executive views:
  of function's roles, 45
  of production, 38
Expediting, 48
Expenses really investments, 43
Experts:
  shifting staff skills, 113

F

Factory costs:
  changes in three decades, 120
  effects of smooth, fast flow, 121
Facts vs. information, 127
Fads, 16
Fallacies, 153
  better to start work sooner, 107
  buying and selling different, 41
  eliminating record errors, 140
  financial manipulations favorable,
    155
  frozen plans, 107
  inventory control, 32
  Japanese unbeatable, 156
  low value dollar needed, 155
  only need know how to read the
      numbers, 37, 99, 122
  poor management major cause of
      U. S. decline, 154
  poor plants can't be competitive,
    38, 62
  problems unsolvable, 109
  professional managers
      unprincipled, 153
  service industries replace
      manufacturing, 26, 154
  U. S. economy strong, 153
  U. S. productivity still leads world,
    154
Feedback:
  timely, 90
  visual better, 129

Finance:
  cultural changes, 99
  primary task, 101
  strategies, 62, 159, 161
Financial measures of performance,
    131
Firefighting, 48
FireKing International Company, 58
First law of manufacturing, 15
  implementation, 19
Flexibility:
  improving, 13
  of resources, 13
Flexible machining systems (FMS),
    83, 94
Flow:
  importance ignored, 8
  information, 7
  materials, 7
Flow Control, 94
Flow lines, 94
Ford, Henry, 9, 40
Ford Motor Company, 106, 110
Foreign competition:
  advantages over U.S. firms, 23
  industries lost to, 22
Freezing plans, 107
Fundamental questions, 89
Future, fertile or futile, 169

G

Galvin, Robert, 163
Geneen, Harold, 18
General Electric Company, 58
General Motors Corporation, 106, 110
Germaine, Jack, 163
Global warming, 158
Globe Metallurgical Company, 163
Group technology, 94

H

Harley-Davidson Company, 154, 160
Harris, Ford, 29

Hierarchy of plans, 54
High precision; dubious accuracy of
    data, 100
Hope for the future, 165
How to read the numbers, 37, 99,
    122

I

IBM, 164
Idle materials:
  causes, 10
  ratio to active, 9
Information flow, 7, 47
  four closed loops, 10
Information vs. facts, 127
Information-based economy, 27
Input/output:
  control, 34, 94
  matching, 108
INSANE cycle, 130
Inspection, 108
Integrated system, 76
Internal control, improving, 92
Inventory:
  asset or liability?, 32
  causes, 131
  control, tank anology, 33
  as cushions, 31
  effective control, 33
  fallacies and truths, 32
  input/output report, 134
  key to control, 33
  not an independent variable, 42
  paradox of control, 33
  potential reductions, 132
  real reductions achieved, 132
  role in business cycles, 33
Inventory turnover:
  best performance measure, 131
  calculating, 131
  Chrysler Corporation, 110
  comparisons dangerous, 131
  Ford Motor Company, 110
  General Motors Corporation,
    110
  realistic goals, 132

Toyota Corporation, 110
Iacocca, Lee, 153

J

JIT (*See* Just-In-Time):
Jobs, Steve, 153
Johnson, H. Thomas, 128
Just-In-Time, 31, 161
    Special Roundtable Report, 18

K

Kroc, Ray, 153

L

Lead time:
    reducing length, 15
    reducing variation, 14
    syndrome, 34
Logic of manufacturing
    answers to questions, 11
    material requirements planning
        application, 80
Long planning horizons, problems
    from, 90
Long range planning, 54

M

Machine tool makers, 30
    still hope for U. S., 4
    why U. S. failing, 3
Malcolm Baldridge National Quality
    Award, 162
Management by objectives, 129
Managements':
    first concern, 88
    handles on the business, 72
Manufacturability, 104
Manufacturers as good citizens, 44
Manufacturing:

common characteristics, 46
compartmentalized view, 45
complexity exaggerated, 6
cycle times, 140
definition, 2
diversity, 44
financial view of, 99
first law of, 15
fundamental objectives, 9
involves two flows, 47
is a process, 40, 51
out of control, 2
primary objectives, 40
role in society, 44
simplifying the process, 92
as strategic weapon, 164
universal logic, 11
Manufacturing Resources Planning
    (MRPII), 97
Marketing and sales:
    cultural changes, 101
    performance measures, 144
    primary task, 101
    role with the master production
        schedule, 102
    strategies, 59, 61, 162
Master planning, 57
Master production schedule
    definition, 68
Master production schedules, 55, 56,
    68
    links to production plans, 67
    managements' role, 72
    questions answered, 68
    typical format, 69
    what they are and are not, 69
Master scheduling, 69
    executive task, 71
    marketings' role, 102
    objectives, 70
    planning not execution, 69
    time periods, 69
Material flow, 7, 9, 47
    glacial pace, 110
    smoothing and speeding, 49
Material requirements planning,
    80
    typical format, 82

Measures of performance (*see*
    Performance measures):
Milliken Company, 163
Modern Materials Handling, 152
Motorola Company, 163
Murphy's Law, 109

N

New product development:
  why so long?, 103
New truths, 110
New United Motors Manufacturing
    Plant, 106
Numbers needed for planning and
    control, 101

O

Overhead costs:
  identifying true causes, 136
  proper allocation, 136
Overloading effects, 98

P

Page, Satchel, 154
Part number uses, 105
Partnerships with suppliers, 112
Performance measures:
  aggregates best, 128
  broad-based, 146
  cost accounting, 146
  customer satisfaction, 41
  focus on vital few, 127
  hierarchy, 130
  for major functions, 144
  means to communicate goals, 147
  plant engineering and
      maintenance, 145
  process engineering, 145
  requirements for effective, 126
  timeliness versus completeness,
    127

visual, 129
Perot, Ross, 153
Peters, Tom, 164
Peters and Waterman, 17
Physical measures of performance,
    138
Physical vs. financial data, 128
Planning:
  criteria for realistic, 48
  definition, 13, 76
  errors, 107
  four levels, 55
  hierarchy, 54
  long range, 54
  purpose, 77
  test of realism, 80
Planning and control evolution, 28, 30
Planning and control systems, 12
  common structure, 12
  core elements, 77
  elements, 12
  multiplant, 75
  objectives, 76
  problems, 37
  reasons for failure, 30
  role of, 12
  serious problems, 37
  subsystems, 82
  universal framework, 77
Plant engineering and maintenance:
  importance in control, 145
  perfomance measures, 145
Pollution, 157
Poor decisions based on:
  book value of machinery, 125
  direct labor efficiency, 122
  direct material costs, 124
  price/earnings ratios, 126
  return on investment, 126
Poor management, first to correct,
    25
Postindustrial:
  economy, 19
  society, 30
Preset tolerances, 91
Prestowitz, Clyde, 151
Preventive maintenance, 113
Price/earning ratios, 126

Primary responsibilities:
  material control, 106
Principles difficult to implement, 168
Priority planning and control, 77
Problems:
  customers' perception, 4
  endemic to manufacturing, 4
  manufacturers' perception, 4
  solvable, 109
  suppliers' perception, 4
  symptoms versus diseases, 48
Process control requirements, 74
Process engineering performance
      measures, 145
Process industry, 49
  Special Interest Group of APICS, 77
Product design:
  simplification, 105
  standardization, 105
Product life cycles, 58
Product profit margins, 135
Production:
  as competitive weapon, 60
  cultural changes, 109
  primary task, 110
  strategies, 59, 61, 161, 164
Production/Delivery Ratio, 139
Production parameters, 147
Production plans, 55, 64
  considerations, 66
  links to master production
      schedules, 67
  objectives, 65
  questions, 64
  steps to develop, 65
  typical format, 66
Production-Sales-Inventory report,
      133
Productivity, 136
  calculating, 136
  financial performance measure,
      136
  France, 154
  improving, 137
  Japan, 154
  physical performance measure, 142
  real gains achieved, 137
  South Korea, 154

  U. S., 154
  West Germany, 154
Profit & loss statement
  after improvement, 166
  before improvement, 166
Profit margin distortions from
      overhead, 119
Profits:
  earning adequate, 42
  not a primary goal, 42
Progress payments, 14
Pull system, 111

Q

Quality control, 108
  basic truths, 108

R

Reducing capital needs, 121
Reducing costs by eliminating
      activities, 120
Replanning, 91
  frequency, 92
  should be last resort, 92
Requirements for effective systems,
      85
Return on asset ratios:
  after improvement, 167
  before improvement, 167
Return on capital employed, 133
Return on investment, 133
Robotics, first test for, 92

S

Safety stock, 31
Sales income versus overhead costs
      curve, 135
Satisfying customers, 119
Schonberger, Richard, 17
Service activities, 26, 155
  not wealth generators, 26

Setup times:
  shortening, 106, 114
Shigeo Shingo, 50
Skinner, Wickham, 60, 61
Smith, Roger, 153
Smith-Corona Division of SCM,
  156
Socialism's failure, 157
Speed of response determines
    benefits, 91
Staff experts changing roles, 113
Standard methods and times
    disadvantages, 105, 123
Standardization, 105
Statistical quality control, 108
Statistical safety stock, 29
Statistics fundamental fallacy, 19
Stockless production, 31
Strategic plans, 55
  content, 62
  questions answered, 57
Strategies:
  attacking waste, 161
  continuous quality improvement,
    162
  design engineering, 60
  finance, 62
  future, 159
  harness computers, 164
  increase capital productivity, 162
  keep resources flexible, 163
  marketing, 59, 61
  need for common, 55, 59
  pounce on discoveries, 164
  production, 59, 61
  speed up flows, 161
  streamline factories, 164
  teamwork, 164
Subsystems, 82
  cost accounting, 84
  customer relations, 84
  demand management, 84
  design engineering, 83
  field service, 85
  internal activities, 83
  invoicing, 85
  plant engineering and
      maintenance, 83

  process engineering, 83
  procurement, 85
  quality control, 83
  supplier relations, 85
  worker performance, 83
Success:
  indicators, 20
Sunset industries, 19

T

Taylor, Frederick W., 122
Teamwork:
  among major functions, 97
  strategies, 164
Technology transfer, 124
Ten Key Standards, 84
Theory of manufacturing, 15
  four corollaries, 15
The Stanley Works, 110
Thompson, G. Lee, 156
Time:
  as resource, 10, 59, 168
  making better use, 11
  periods of supply, 138
  waste is heinous crime, 10
Total quality control, 161
Toyota Company, 106, 110
Traditional:
  accounting systems, problems
      with, 118
  measures of performance, 118

U

U. S. economic power:
  causes of decline, 22, 150
  financial handicaps, 24, 151
  government handicaps, 23, 151
  poor management handicaps, 25
  prerequisites for healthy, 19
  union handicaps, 24
U. S. industry evolution since
    WW II, 28
U. S. Japan trade relations, 25

U. S. machine tool makers, 3
U. S. News & World Report, 162

V

Valid plans:
  characteristics, 89
  relation to time horizon, 13

W

Wall Street Journal, 164
Waste:
  causes, 50
  definition, 50
Watson, Tom, Sr., 164
Wealth generation:
  vs. distribution, 27
  governments' share, 27
  importance of manufacturing, 26
  managers' share, 27
  owners' share, 27

sharing equitably, 43
suppliers' share, 27
three ways, 26
value added is not, 43
workers' share, 27
Wilson, R. H., 29
Workers:
  not commodities, 161
  as resource, 159
Work-in-process, 8
World class competitor
  goals, 40
  requirements, 38

X

Xerox Corporation, 163

Z

Zero defects, 108, 160, 163